D0667368

*TWAYNE'S WORLD AUTHORS SERIES*

*A Survey of the World's Literature*

Sylvia E. Bowman, Indiana University
GENERAL EDITOR

# SOUTH AFRICA

Joseph Jones, University of Texas
EDITOR

## Laurens van der Post

*(TWAS 68)*

# TWAYNE'S WORLD AUTHORS SERIES (TWAS)

*The purpose of TWAS is to survey the major writers —novelists, dramatists, historians, poets, philosophers, and critics—of the nations of the world. Among the national literatures covered are those of Australia, Canada, China, Eastern Europe, France, Germany, Greece, India, Italy, Japan, Latin America, New Zealand, Poland, Russia, Scandinavia, Spain, and the African nations, as well as Hebrew, Yiddish, and Latin Classical literatures. This survey is complemented by Twayne's United States Authors Series and English Authors Series.*

*The intent of each volume in these series is to present a critical-analytical study of the works of the writer; to include biographical and historical material that may be necessary for understanding, appreciation, and critical appraisal of the writer; and to present all material in clear, concise English—but not to vitiate the scholarly content of the work by doing so.*

# Laurens van der Post

By FREDERIC I. CARPENTER
University of California at Berkeley

Twayne Publishers, Inc.  ::  New York

LIBRARY
WAYNE STATE COLLEGE
Wayne, Nebraska

*Copyright © 1969, by Twayne Publishers, Inc.*
All Rights Reserved

Library of Congress Catalog Card Number: 68-17236

MANUFACTURED IN THE UNITED STATES OF AMERICA

For Dixie

134953

# Acknowledgments

I am deeply grateful to Mr. Laurens van der Post for his kind assistance in the preparation of this book, and for his permission to quote from unpublished letters. For similar assistance, I am grateful to Mr. William Plomer, and Mr. T. C. Robertson.

I acknowledge permission of the following authors and publishers to quote from published books: Laurens van der Post, and his publishers, William Morrow and Co. (New York), and The Hogarth Press (London), for all his books. William Plomer, and The Noonday Press (New York), *Double Lives*. Desmond Young, and Harper and Row (New York), *All the Best Years*. Frank Debenham, and Bell (London), *Kalahari Sand*. Ezekiel Mphahlele, and Frederick A. Praeger (New York), *The African Image*. Loren Eiseley, and Random House (New York), *The Immense Journey*. All authors, and editors of magazines, for articles and pamphlets listed individually in "Notes and References."

# Preface

Until five years ago I had never read anything by Laurens van der Post. Then I read *Venture to the Interior*, and soon after that all the books that he had written. The more I read the more fascinated I became, until one day as I was driving across the Bay Bridge from San Francisco, I found myself conducting a dialogue with him on the front seat of my car. It seemed a natural thing to do, because he had entered into my imagination so completely that I felt him as a close friend. Some time later, when I had contracted to do this book about him, I wrote to ask his help, ' and he replied generously. Later he visited Berkeley to give a lecture at the University of California, and as we drove across the Bay Bridge in my car, our dialogue seemed not too different from what I had imagined earlier. The man is very like his books.

I recall this experience because it suggests answers to some important questions, both about van der Post and about this book. Friends have asked why, after thirty years of reading and writing about American authors, I suddenly became interested in a South African? Or, negatively, why did I consider myself qualified to write this book about a South African? The answer, of course, is that he did not seem like a foreigner, and this book does not describe him primarily as a South African, but as a world figure. Chapter 1 tells of his early life in South Africa, and suggests parallels between South African history and American. But at the age of twenty-one he left South Africa, and since then has become progressively a citizen of the world.

I use the words "world figure" and "citizen of the world" rather than "world author." Although this book is one of a "World Authors Series," only two chapters (Four and Five) discuss his books individually. The first half of this book narrates the life of van der Post, the man. I have gone against all the traditions of modern criticism to emphasize the individual man who has created the books, and have relegated the books to second place. This is, partly, because his life has been extraordinarily active

7

and interesting in itself. Partly, it is because all his books have
been autobiographical, some of them factually and some figura-
tively. But chiefly, this is because his life and his books have
interacted to create a new kind of autobiographical personality,
or literary legend, which may be greater than either his life or
his books.

When I first read these books, I read them all at once; and
when I had finished reading, I remembered not the individual
books, but rather the man who had both experienced and written them. And of course I did not "remember" the man (whom
I had not yet met), but the autobiographical personality which
the man had created, partly by means of the books. This created
personality had so captured my imagination that he had become
more real than reality. And this extraordinary experience raised
echoes in my mind: I remembered the earlier experience of
reading Walt Whitman ("Who touches this book touches a
man"), when the created personality had also overshadowed the
book and overwhelmed the imagination. And I remembered the
books of Thomas Wolfe, whose novels—even if they were not
novels—had also created an autobiographical personality larger
than literature and more real than life. These literary experiences
seemed all of a kind.

These literary experiences—and others of the same kind but of
a lesser magnitude—suggested, paradoxically, a new theory of
literary criticism. For the "new criticism" of our older generation has always emphasized that each book must be read and
judged on its own merits as an individual work of literary art.
But some typically modern authors have spent their lives writing a series of books which create cumulatively a single life-
work-of-art, which is greater than the sum of its parts and to
which each individual part refers. Sometimes self-consciously,
as with Whitman's "Song of Myself," and sometimes by half-
conscious compulsion, as with the gigantic novels of Thomas
Wolfe, these modern writers have created a new kind of autobiographical hero, part history and part myth. In the process
they have rejected the formal patterns of traditional art and
criticism in order to create their unique literary personalities.

As this idea gradually became clear, I realized that this South
African author and his autobiographical personality had fascinated me partly because he and his books had repeated a pat-

tern which had formerly seemed typically American. Where all European authors have shared a relatively homogeneous cultural tradition, Americans have experienced an immense variety and confusion of cultures: after leaving their ancestral homes in Europe and coming to a new world peopled with savages, Americans founded a new nation with mixed heritages. And some American writers have sought to define their new American identities by imagining new "selves" in terms of an ideal American personality: so Whitman imagined an ideal democratic "myself" chanting a "barbaric yawp" in the new world, and Wolfe created a new, autobiographical Eugene Gant as the American seeker. And just so, perhaps, Laurens van der Post, born of Boer ancestry in the African interior between the conquered Blacks and the recently conquering British, and living through a greater variety of events in a greater confusion of cultures than any American, has created his own autobiographical personality, partly in terms of biographical fact, and partly of literary imagination.

The concept of an autobiographical myth, created in response to the pioneer experiences of modern man on new continents and in a collision of many cultures, is too large to be defined here. But the concept, or the literary experience which suggested it, has determined the form of this book. Reinforced by similar experiences of other readers of van der Post, it has led to an emphasis on the personality or character of the man. The autobiographical personality dominates this book.

Chapter 1 narrates the biography of the author in so far as it has had to do with his native Africa: it includes events and experiences of this past year, as well as of his ancestry and early life there. Chapter 2 tells of his middle years: the early period of dislocation and "exile" in England before the war, and then the war years crammed with violent experience both outer and inner. Chapter 3 narrates the sudden rush of creative activity which followed the war, and the emergence of the world figure, both in terms of authorship and of actual life.

Chapters 4 and 5 describe and criticize the books individually. Chapter 4 discusses the non-fiction: it is perhaps the more interesting because the non-fiction has been the more successful. It suggests the structural metaphor of "The Immense Journey" to describe the unity of form and of meaning underlying both the

life and the books. Chapter 5 discusses the novels, and suggests
their unity in terms of the metaphor of "The Heart of Darkness."
These borrowed titles may both describe their subject matter
and suggest their literary and psychological significance.

Finally, Chapter 6 explores the techniques by which the author
has realized his autobiographical myth, first in life and then in
literature. It relates this myth to the historic patterns of
African life, and to the ideal patterns of philosophy and psychology which lie behind. It attempts to project a single "African
Myth," in order to explain the fascination of Africa and of
van der Post's books for the modern reader. In conclusion, it
seeks to judge these books as literature. The final chapter adds
little new information, but may suggest the originality and
challenge of the author's writing.

FREDERIC I. CARPENTER

*Berkeley, California*

# *Contents*

# Contents

# Chronology

1835– "The Great Trek." His mother's grandfather and party mas-
1837  sacred by the Matabele.

1899– The Boer War. His father on commando, captured by the
1902  British.

1906  Laurens Jan van der Post born, December 13, near Philip-
      polis, Orange Free State.

1914  His father died.

1914– Attended local schools.
1920

1920– Grey College School, Bloemfontein.
1925

1925– Reporter on the *Natal Advertiser*, Durban.
1926

1926  Contributed to *Voorslag*. Voyage to Japan on the *Canada
      Maru*, and return.

1928  Moved to London. Married Marjorie Wendt.

1929  Contributed to *The Realist*. Son, Jan Laurens van der Post,
      born.

1930  Leader writer for the *Cape Times*, South Africa.

1934  First novel, *In a Province*, published. Bought farm in Glou-
      cestershire.

1936  Daughter, Lucia van der Post, born.

1939  Enlisted, and training as commando.

1940  Served as officer in Abyssinia behind the Italian lines.

1941  Commando, North Africa and Syria.

1942  Commando, Sumatra and Java. Captured by the Japanese.

1942– Prisoner of war of the Japanese in Java.
1945

1945  Brief return to England, and mission to The Netherlands.

13

1945– On staff of British minister, Batavia (Djakarta).
1947

1947   Return to England. Commander, Order of the British
       Empire.

1948   Editor, *Natal Daily News.*

1949   Government mission to Nyasaland. Divorced Marjorie
       Wendt. Married Ingaret Giffard.

1950– Government missions to the Kalahari.
1952

1951   *Venture to the Interior* published in America (in England,
       1952).

1953   *The Face Beside the Fire.* His mother died.

1954   *A Bar of Shadow* (first published in *The Cornhill,* 1952).

1955   *Flamingo Feather. The Dark Eye in Africa.* Private expe-
       dition to the Kalahari.

1956   Film, "The Lost World of the Kalahari," issued by the
       British Broadcasting Company. First visit to America
       (December).

1958   *The Lost World of the Kalahari* published.

1961   *The Heart of the Hunter.*

1963   *The Seed and the Sower.*

1964   *A View of All the Russias* (English title: *Journey into
       Russia*). Honorary degree, University of Natal.

1965   "Introduction" to new edition of *Turbott Wolfe,* by Wil-
       liam Plomer.

1967   *The Hunter and the Whale.*

# PART ONE: THE MAN

## CHAPTER 1

# Van der Post of Africa

### I    History and Myth

MOST of the books of Laurens van der Post describe the life and the problems of the continent of Africa, past, present and future. Many narrate in factual detail the historic experiences of his ancestors as pioneers in South Africa, and the autobiographical experiences of his own youth there. *Venture to the Interior* tells of the massacre of his mother's grandfather and his party in the wild country beyond the Vaal River during the Great Trek, and (two generations later) of the capture of his father by the British on commando near the end of the Boer War. *The Lost World of the Kalahari* describes his own childhood life among the Bushman and Bantu servants of his father's ranch to explain his lifelong fascination with the history of the aboriginal people and with their present fate. And in *The Dark Eye in Africa* he makes a confession of faith: "At heart I am indelibly and irrevocably in and of Africa.... Much as I love Europe, I am continually being reminded that the master pattern at work within me, the magnet which conditions the field of all my reactions, is African."

With such a background of history and experience, and so strong a feeling of belonging heart and soul to his native continent, it is natural that he should have become one of its most eloquent interpreters. And as the "dark continent" has emerged in recent years into the bright light of contemporary history, his fame has spread throughout the world. Like his life-long friend, William Plomer, with whom he shared apprenticeship to the career of author in Durban, he can say, "I Speak of Africa." More perhaps than any official spokesman he can add, "I speak for Africa." For he has always sought to give expression to the problems and feelings of its disenfranchised and often inarticulate peoples.

Obviously his own life has prepared him for this role of spokesman, and his autobiographical writing has emphasized this. The story of the life of his ancestors in Africa has helped illustrate its past history. These facts are important to the understanding of his books. But beyond the mere facts of biography and of history, he has drawn upon a vast background of African lore and legend. What gives new dimension to his interpretations of modern Africa is his knowledge and love of its timeless myths. Before his earliest ancestors settled the land of South Africa—before history, there was myth.

In his recent "Introduction" to William Plomer's early novel of black Africa, *Turbott Wolfe*, van der Post recalls a passage from *The Lusiad* by the Portuguese Camoens, which describes in mythical terms the first historic Portuguese exploration of Africa and the East.

Camoens tells how one calm clear evening off the cape [of Good Hope], Vasco da Gama, alone on deck, is over-awed by a sudden darkening of the sky. He looks up and sees a gigantic black shape with negroid features towering over his ship. The gigantic shape booms at him, "I am the spirit of this far-flung and much tormented Cape.". . .The black shape explains that he is the last of the Titans, that he has dared to love a white nymph and daughter of the God of the Sea who had been promised to him because of the help he had given the Gods in their struggle against the Titans. When the battle was over she was denied him and his love of this nymph, white with the foam and spray of the sea, was regarded as so grave a presumption that he was bound to the Cape and turned to stone. The black giant then tells Vasco da Gama that a day will come when the Portuguese will be called to account and severely punished for having broken so brutally into the remote worlds of the East. Here, in the form of a poetic intuition and parable, is the history of Africa. The black man received from the European many gifts, but . . . the black man was denied the white love of which Camoens' nymph is the image, and in the process his heart was turned to stone.[1]

This "poetic intuition and parable" seems more important to van der Post than prosaic history.

Among modern South African authors, van der Post has valued the fantastic adventure novels of H. Rider Haggard more highly than most. And in Haggard's most famous and most fantastic novel, *She* (1887), the modern hero also sails the Coast of Africa in search of an ageless white nymph, who, although once queen of ancient Egypt and once wed to the classical Greek Kallikrates, now rules a kingdom in the unknown interior of the dark continent. This modern hero is shipwrecked in Portuguese Mozambique at the foot of a "peak, about eighty feet high by one hundred and fifty feet thick at its base, shaped like a negro's head and face, whereon was stamped a most fiendish and terrifying expression." But the modern hero now ventures into the dark interior, to confront the beautiful white Ayesha, the ageless young queen who rules over her black subjects with absolute power.

Although these mythical imaginings may be fantastic, they suggest a truth more important than history. Better, they suggest a truth of which history is only one part. For they recall that Africa itself was once the birthplace of civilization, and that modern African history is only one phase of an age-old process, whose intermediate steps have been lost and forgotten. Somewhere in the sands of upper Egypt or beyond the sources of the Nile this early African civilization was buried, but it has persisted in racial memories as a kind of myth, which also prophesies some future renewal and return. The white queen Ayesha becomes the symbol of the ancient African impulse toward civilization lost to history in the timeless interior. And Adamastor— the black cloud-shape which threatened Vasco da Gama, like the black cliff-head that threatened the fictional English explorer of Rider Haggard—becomes the symbol of this thwarted impulse, now harshly rejected by the European. Significantly, this mythical black titan had sought to give help to the gods in their war against the titans, only to be rejected.

These myths are vague. But they prophesy both the pattern of van der Post's writing, and of modern African history. The myth of the white queen suggests, optimistically, the future acceptance of civilization by black Africa, and recalls the first impulse toward civilization which had flowered in North Africa.

Documenting this myth, van der Post has described the painting of an ideal white queen which he saw on a rock-wall in the Kalahari, together with the painting of a white lotus-flower unknown to actual Africa. And he has told of seeing the ritual enactment of classical myths, such as that of the pipes of Pan in Abyssinia, and the cupid's bow in the Kalahari. Most important, he has actually explored the culture of the aboriginal African Bushmen, in order to describe their artistic rituals and dances, and to collect and interpret their myths.

Opposing the optimistic myth of the timeless white queen ruling the savage interior, stands the pessimistic myth of the threatening Negro cloud-shape or cliff-head. Historically, van der Post has described the feelings of guilt which this threatening shape symbolizes, in the historic life of his people, and he has sought to expiate this guilt by his own devotion to the Bushmen. *The Dark Eye in Africa* may be read, autobiographically, as his own interpretation of this pessimistic myth of white guilt and black hostility, applied to modern African life. Finally, his own lifelong opposition to the principle and practice of *apartheid* illustrates his practical realization of the idea behind this myth. He has sought to give the black titan of Africa the gift of the love of the mythical white queen.

These myths suggest endless avenues of interpretation: the final chapter of this book will explore some of them. Here it is only important to remember their existence, and the fact that van der Post has always valued them. He has sought to collect the unwritten myths of the African aborigines and to interpret them. He has described and interpreted the myths about Africa, both oral and written, which Europeans have imagined. But most important is his interest in myth itself, which has resulted in his development of its symbolic patterns in his own writing. "The master-pattern at work within me" has been shaped not only by African history, but by African myth.

## II  *Trek and War*

Against this background of myth, the history of modern South Africa has played itself out. And history as we know it began in South Africa in 1652, almost a century after the death of Camoens, when the first European settlers landed at the Cape of Good Hope. Among these were van der Post's maternal ancestors, and although he has not traced their genealogy, many of his books remember their spirit.

*The Lost World of the Kalahari* achieves a hauntingly vivid re-creation of early South African history, and identifies the author with it. But it also emphasizes the total violence of that history, and the ruthless warfare by which his ancestors exterminated the aboriginal Bushman hunters, much as American pioneers exterminated the Indian hunters. And the totality of this violence was motivated by the same religious spirit which motivated our New England ancestors: "If there was a conscience at work," van der Post writes, "it was submerged in the labyrinthine basement of the Calvinistic spirit of my people." Like many modern American authors, he has felt deeply the blood-guilt of his ancestors, and has sought a kind of atonement for it in his writing.

But if the Calvinistic spirit of the pioneers was sometimes an instrument of destruction, it was also an instrument of creation which fortified them against hardship and despair. Many of his books remember the hymns the Dutch Calvinists sang, not only in church, but also on their treks and military campaigns. The memory of his mother's churchgoing is bound up with the memory of her goodness. And although he has repudiated the intolerance of Calvinist doctrine, he has founded his life on the deeper Christian faith which underlay it.

The pioneer history of South Africa, which so closely parallels the pioneer history of America, diverges from it with the domination of the Dutch settlers by the British in 1795. Although the American New Amsterdam became New York by easy transition, South African history was punctuated by skirmishes between the Dutch and the British. And to escape from British domination, the Boers organized the Great Trek to the Northern interior in 1835–37. Throughout the nineteenth century they struggled to re-establish their independence of the British. The Boer War, from 1899 to 1902, merely marked the culmination of a long series of incidents and lesser wars.

Therefore the pattern of South African history, which has so profoundly influenced van der Post, differs radically from the American. Throughout American history the simple conflict of pioneers and Indians prevailed, so that our traditional "West-

erns" have always celebrated the simplistic opposition of the
"good guys" and the "bad guys." But in South Africa the Boers
have traditionally fought the native black peoples on the one
side, and on the other, the British. Against this double danger
the Boer has drawn upon his Calvinistic religion in order to
preserve his freedom and his identity. Through the centuries
this triple conflict between Boer, Briton, and Black African has
continued to disturb the young men.

The importance of the story of van der Post's ancestry and
early life lies in its vivid illustration of the common experiences
of South African history. But the fascination of his later life lies
in its divergence from the norms of that history. In retelling the
adventures of his grandparents, for instance, he emphasizes the
archetypal nature of their experiences. "The Journey in Time,"
which introduces *Venture to the Interior*, describes how his
great-grandfather's party "had moved in the forefront of a vast
exodus," forming "part of the great trek of Dutch farmers from
British rule at the Cape." And "the incoherent account in broken
Afrikaans given by the half-caste maid" of the massacre of the
party, and of her own rescue of his grandmother from the Matabele, emphasizes the legendary nature of the event. From all
this "ill-fated Liebenberg Trek," fleeing from the British in the
South only to be ambushed by Black tribesmen in the North,
only his grandmother and her baby brother and sister were saved
by a half-caste nurse.

As in all van der Post's books of non-fiction, the autobiographical events described are fundamentally accurate. But the exact
details are sometimes blurred by memory and sometimes re-
ordered by art. Thus he has recently corrected the story of the
massacre, writing:

I made a mistake in my description in *Venture to the Interior*, pointed
out to me when the book appeared by my mother. Liebenberg was
the name of my mother's grandfather. He went far ahead of the main
body of the first trekers and camped one night almost on the banks of
the Vaal. In the night the wagons were surrounded by the Matabele.
The children owed their lives to the fact that they were naughty,
because they woke very early and were so noisy that my mother's
grandfather could not sleep. He ordered the maid to take them down
to the river. My grandmother, her sister and her brother had just
reached the river with their nurse when the Matabele attacked and

massacred the sleeping laga. There were, therefore, not two child survivors, as I said, but three. The scene of the massacre is commemorated to this day by two hills, called the Liebenberg Koppies.[2]

After the Liebenberg massacre and the end of the Great Trek, the Boer settlers continued to fight against both Black Africans and British. Van der Post's maternal grandfather was captured by the British at the Battle of Boomplatz in 1848. His father, in turn, was captured by the British while on commando toward the end of the Boer War." He was the second prisoner of war in my family, I was the third." War has always remained a constant through South African history. And to be captured by superior force at the end of battle has been honor rather than disgrace. This ancestral pattern of Afrikaner life was to determine van der Post's individual life a generation later, in a greater war in a stranger country.

The Boer—officially "the South African War"—was itself a very strange kind of war. Mark Twain happened to be visiting South Africa at that time, at the end of his long travels *Following the Equator,* and described the famous "Jameson Raid" which began the war. It seemed to him a confused kind of comic opera affair. But from within the comic opera must have seemed more like nightmare, and the calculated duplicity of Cecil Rhodes seemed more like treachery to the Boers. A generation later the Englishman William Plomer would describe the machinations of Rhodes with indignant scorn.[3] And the idea of manifest destiny, which the Americans had invoked earlier to excuse their own conquest of uncivilized and underpopulated countries, could hardly be used to excuse the British suppression of the Boer Republics.

"For two years," van der Post writes, "my father was out on Commando." More than a generation later he himself was to be "out on commando" for three years. More than "trek" or "war," the word "commando" suggests the element of South African history which dominated the pattern of van der Post's early life. For "commando" is in origin an Afrikaner word, later adopted by British and American usage, and acquiring a slightly different meaning in each country. Now it usually means a military unit (or soldier in that unit) conducting raids behind enemy lines. But in South Africa it originally meant a military unit raised for protection against marauding attackers. Through the massacres and countermarches of South African history, Boer

commandos fought to protect their families and their settle-
ments from the Blacks and the British alike. Only after a century of wars, half Black and half British, did the Boer suffer
final conquest by the British empire at the end of the South
African War.

### III  *Boer or British?*

Laurens van der Post's father, Christian Willem Hendrik van
der Post, had been a leader of the Orange Free State both before
and during the Boer War, and his life profoundly influenced his
son. After the war his struggle to reconcile himself to British
domination, and later to identify himself with that political
"Union" of South Africa, which attempted also to realize the psychological union of Boer and British loyalties, became the fundamental struggle of his son's early life also. As citizens of a
conquered nation they both faced the problem: did loyalty lie
with the Boer past, or with the British future? Laurens inherited
this conflict of loyalties—this problem of identity—and all of his
life and much of his writing have been devoted to its solution.
The problem of reconciliation to defeat, and the much greater
problem of the transcendence of defeat, has been central to all
his thinking.

He has told the story of his father's and his mother's lives in
Part I of *Venture to the Interior*. Reminiscences of his parents
and childhood recur in *The Kalahari* and *The Dark Eye*. The
characters of his father and mother are transformed into fictional
patterns in *The Face Beside the Fire*, but mixed with elements
from the lives and characters of his grandparents as well. There
is no need to retell these stories, except as they illuminate the
problems of his own writing.

Before the Boer War, his father had been chairman of the
Executive Council of the Parliament of the Orange Free State
Republic. After the war, his father's bitterness against the British
made him refuse British citizenship, and choose confinement and
exile. In exile he wrote "two novels about South Africa's itinerant
past, partly in Dutch and partly in Afrikaans." After "Campbell-
Bannerman's great gesture of reconciliation," he worked happily
with the British for the Union of greater South Africa. But further hostility between the peoples forced him at last to abandon
politics, and to retire again to exile. On his own great farm he

died in August, 1914, on the day that the Great War began in Europe.

Like his father, Laurens van der Post would write novels during his own years of psychological exile from the inherited bitterness of South African politics. But he would not write them in Afrikaans, and he would recall his South African past, not for nostalgia, but for illumination of the problems of the present. And he would choose "exile," not for retirement, but for perspective. "The doctors said he [my father] died of double pneumonia," he wrote. "I know he died of exile." Although he himself has struggled all his life with the inherited problem of alienation, or "exile," he has increasingly transcended it.

An interview published in the *Cape Times*,[4] the leading English newspaper of South Africa, has recalled his early life: "Laurens van der Post as a child inherited the almost automatic mistrust of everything British that seemed to be the inevitable legacy of all Afrikaner children of his day. He says it was not until he managed to walk out of that bitterness and saw it as a something that belonged to history and not the present or the future, that he began to feel and think like an individual human being." But this problem of individuation has proved not quite so simple. Although he "managed to walk out of that bitterness," which had destroyed his father, his own lifelong "venture to the interior" has been the result of "a growing realization that somehow my life must find a way out between my father's exile and my mother's home."

As a child, the problem of language came first. Until he was seven, he spoke only Afrikaans. He did not learn English until he was ten. His first publication was poetry written in Afrikaans in a local journal. His first serious essays were also written in Afrikaans. Even now he is most at home in Afrikaans and says that he often thinks in it. Although he feels himself "essentially a poet," he has never written poetry in English, because he believes that poetry (unlike prose) can only be written in one's own native language. Indeed, he learned to read French and German books of his father's library almost as soon as English. And to this day he both speaks and reads these languages with great fluency.

He learned English, therefore, as a secondary language. And he learned it for literary reasons even more than for practical ones. His father had always been a lover of literature, but in spite of his father's novels, Afrikaans was not yet a literary language. Even the High Dutch in which the church services of his youth were conducted had been poor in fine literature. But as he went through school, first in the village where he was born, and later to the Grey College School in Bloemfontein, he experienced the native Boer prejudice against the English language as the symbol of British domination. The teacher with whom he boarded while in Bloemfontein tried to argue him out of his enthusiasm for this alien language. Yet his love for English literature, reinforced by the necessity of proficiency in English for life in the larger world, prevailed. And as he grew up he increasingly acquired both proficiency and eloquence in the alien language.

This internal conflict between natural loyalty to the Boer past, and acquired recognition of the necessity of Union with the British, can hardly be overestimated. In this conflict the Boer identified with loyalty to the soil ("Boer" means "peasant"), to the family, and to the conservative traditions of the pioneer past. But these loyalties conflicted with the ways of British and cosmopolitan culture, of industrialism, and the philosophies of the modern world. Of course this conflict of loyalties was worldwide, as he has emphasized in *The Dark Eye*. But the South African history of national and racial antagonisms sharpened it to the extreme.

Beyond history and biography, however, van der Post's novels have objectified this inner conflict by projecting it upon two opposite pairs of brothers (or foster-brothers). The artist-hero of *The Face Beside the Fire* flees from South Africa to England because of conflict with his parents, while his foster-brother remains at home with his traditional family. And in *The Seed and the Sower*, the handsome, blond brother rejects his deformed dark brother (who loves farming and the soil), and leaves to win glory in the larger world. But in each case the cosmopolitan brother can achieve happiness only by reconciliation with his opposite.

## IV  An African Farm

Together with the conflict between Boer and Briton which he inherited from South African history and from his father, he inherited the greater conflict between African and European loyalties from both his parents. "Africa is my mother's country," he wrote at the beginning of his *Venture to the Interior;* but his father's loyalty had remained with Europe. And this greater conflict continued to dominate his own life.

After his mother's mother had been rescued from the Liebenberg massacre, she had married a successful Afrikaner pioneer named Lubbe. And from them his own mother, Maria Magdalena Lubbe, had inherited a large African farm. On this farm, near Philippolis, she had married, and here she reared her family of fifteen children. The thirteenth of these, born on December 13, 1906, was Laurens van der Post. But after her husband's death in 1914, and after the last children had grown up and left home, she too left the ancestral farm, and at the age of seventy moved to a remote farm, which had been allowed to run down. Then once again, at the age of eighty, she ventured farther into the interior to develop new land on the very edge of the Kalahari Desert. Her youngest son was to inherit from this mother both the ancestral farm where he had been born, and the indomitable pioneer love of exploration.

This ancestral farm of the van der Posts exerted an influence on his life almost greater than that of his parents. His books recall many vivid incidents from this life: the herding of cattle on the ranges, the ceremony of shearing the sheep, the hunting of wild animals, and the care of a variety of tame pets, the black Basuto workers and the mixed household retainers, and above all the land—as wild as that of the American West, and even more vivid under the bright blue of the subtropical sky. Most simply, this farm represented a way of life and a means of income. As a boy he performed the chores of farm life, and loved it. His books all describe this life with a sense of active participation, rather than mere observation. And although he soon left the farm for school, and later to write for newspapers, and still later to create his own books, he always remained a farmer at heart. After moving to London and becoming a man of letters, he suddenly abandoned the literary community there and bought a new farm of his own in Gloucestershire, which he farmed individually for four years. And long after World War II, when he was touring Soviet Russia as a journalist, he was able to criticize the spokesman of a Russian collective—not for his

theories of collective farming, but for his techniques of breed-
ing cattle.

Beyond the practical values of farming and of identification
with the good earth, the ancestral farm came also to symbolize
a sense of citizenship, and of continuity in a changing world.
After the children had all left, and after the parents had died,
the farm was divided among the descendants. And later, as each
of the descendants either died or lost interest in the land,
Laurens reacquired most of it, and has kept it in trust for the
family. Although now living in London, he still lists "Wolwekop,
Philippolis, South Africa," as one of his permanent homes and
still conducts the business of the farm, partly by means of representatives who visit him in England and partly by occasional
visits of his own to the farm. He still remains legally a citizen of
the Union of South Africa, and still "commutes between England
and South Africa," in the pursuit of his official business as active
farmer. Amidst the confusion of political loyalties, the changing
techniques of industrial life, and the abstraction of a life of
letters, this ancestral African farm still provides a symbol of
permanence.

But the chief significance of this farm probably lies in its
African-ness, rather than its agricultural way of life or temporal
value. The English farm which he bought had never felt like
home. And as he grew older he increasingly realized that his
chief loyalties were African. But what did "African" loyalty
really mean?

The first important book to interpret modern South African
life had been *The Story of an African Farm* (1883), by Olive
Schreiner. "With her," van der Post writes, "English literature
in South Africa suddenly becomes profoundly indigenous and
the imagination is native."[5] Moreover, Olive Schreiner's book
might almost have described the actual setting of van der Post's
own farm, for she had actually lived several years in the town
of Philippolis. "To this day I see in the themes and the words
she chose, this village and its surroundings . . ." The hard pioneer
life, and the puritanical Afrikaner spirit found such vivid expression in this book of an earlier generation that it appealed to
the modern author as profoundly "African." But, he wrote, "there
is a curious limitation upon her awareness: the black and coloured people of Africa, who were with her from birth and far

outnumbered the white, are not naturally and immediately in it."

The more he read African literature and thought about African life, comparing books like Olive Schreiner's *Story of an African Farm* with his own childhood memories of life on his own African farm, the more he realized that every African farm was more than African land, and more than Afrikaner (or English) owners. "An African Farm" included more black and coloured people than white. And "African loyalty" (as opposed to European loyalty) was loyalty to the total life and experience of Africa, black and white.

As he grew older his mind recalled increasingly the total experience of his childhood life on his farm. *Venture to the Interior* recalled how all the black and coloured workers, "in defiance of the cold convention already being thrust on the country by self-conscious patriots from the Cape," had insisted on calling his mother by the familiar name, "The Little Lamb." *The Lost World of the Kalahari* remembered how his Bushman nurse had told him tales of her own aboriginal African people. And *The Dark Eye* recalled that "moment of innocence," now lost, when briefly Black African and White had lived together without dark suspicion and hatred. Seeking to recapture that lost moment, he later journeyed to "The Lost World of the Kalahari."

After writing his book about the Kalahari, he spent several years wondering how to dramatize his realization of the totality of that African world of his childhood, where "all who worked for my grandfather, no matter whether Griqua, Hottentot, Bushman, Basuto, Bechuana, Cape-coloured or poor white, were ultimately held in equal affection." By contrast, *The Heart of the Hunter* now described how he saw a contemporary gang of young Afrikaner boys beat up a single Negro boy without reason. Then, remembering his own early affection for his own black playmates, he also remembered the sudden break when he had been sent to a segregated white school. Organized society had created the break—both between his own childhood experience of a united Africa and his later separation from Black Africa; and between the "moment of innocence" of historic African life, and the dark hatred engendered by formal segregation. In the words of the American song: "You've got to be carefully taught." After having learned as a young man to accept the South African "Union" between Boer and British, his

books have progressively sought to recapture that greater Union
between Black and White, which his own "African Farm" had
once realized.

## V  Voorslag

Grey College School, which young van der Post attended in
Bloemfontein, was the South African equivalent of a British
public school, or an American preparatory school. It was conservative, conventional, and of course segregated. Its life was
almost the exact opposite of the life to which he had been
accustomed on the African farm of his childhood. He attended
it continuously till his graduation in 1925. But then he termi-
nated his formal education. On graduating he did not continue
to college like most of his classmates, but left home and sought
work as a journalist.

He has vividly described the privileged life of this type of
school in an early episode of *The Seed and the Sower*. In this
novel the first-person hero succeeds brilliantly, while his unfor-
tunate "twin" brother suffers intensely from the social snobbish-
ness and cruelty of the place. In his own life, however, he experienced both success and unhappiness at Grey College School.
He enjoyed success when his natural athletic prowess made him
a leader among his fellows, but various academic experiences
caused him difficulty—both real and psychological. A few teach-
ers befriended and inspired him, but others (including the
headmaster) disliked and disapproved of him. His difficulties
were caused partly by his love of European literature, and his
wide but undisciplined reading in it—to the detriment of his
formal courses. But he also wrote some unorthodox articles for
the school paper, one of which (entitled "An Interview with
God") almost got him expelled. As his career developed, he
progressively lost interest in formal studies and might not even
have graduated except for his skill at games and his popularity
among his fellow students.

In 1925 he left his native Orange Free State and went to
Durban, seeking work as a journalist. After being turned down
by all the Afrikaans newspapers because he lacked a university
degree, he was accepted by the English-language *Natal Advertiser* because of his ability to write English. His first article,
entitled "The Superstition of Examinations in South Africa," was

quickly published, and marks the beginning of his professional career. For about a year he continued as reporter on the *Advertiser,* in spite of frequent disagreements with the editor.

He has told the story of this period in his "Introduction" (written forty years later) to the 1965 edition of William Plomer's early novel, *Turbott Wolfe.* And *Turbott Wolfe,* first published in the spring of 1926, profoundly influenced him. For the first time in South African history, this novel dared to imagine a happy marriage between a white woman and a black man. But of course this situation outraged the conventional society of the country. The *Natal Advertiser* published an editorial damning the novel, and van der Post replied with a series of letters (which the paper duly published without censorship) defending it. Through his public advocacy of this unpopular book, he met the author—a young man only three years older than he. And their meeting began a lifelong friendship, which changed the courses of the lives of both men, and which has influenced the lives and writing of other South African authors.

When van der Post and Plomer first met in Durban, Plomer and his friend Roy Campbell had just founded a new magazine, entitled *Voorslag.* The program of this magazine immediately attracted van der Post. It planned to publish articles, poetry, and fiction, not only in English, but in Afrikaans and in Zulu, by writers representing all the races of South Africa. Because Plomer and Campbell were both English, they welcomed van der Post as an author whose native language was Afrikaans. They invited him to visit them at Roy Campbell's home in the country, and the three talked for days almost without sleep, projecting the future course of the magazine, and of their writing.

Both van der Post and Plomer[6] have described the excitement of this new venture, and of their discussions together, and there is no need to repeat their stories. But the significance of this magazine and of their friendship is greater than that of their individual lives and books. Although *Voorslag* published a total of only eleven issues, and reached comparatively few readers, it achieved a literary and historical importance roughly equivalent to that of the American transcendentalist magazine, *The Dial.* The later fame of its editors resembles that of Emerson and Thoreau, and, like *The Dial, Voorslag* gave expression to a clear and important literary program and philosophy.

Roy Campbell, the son of a Durban physician, was the prime mover in establishing *Voorslag*. He first enlisted the financial backing for it, and—when the timid backers objected to the radical articles which appeared in the first two issues—he in turn rejected their conditions, and resigned, dooming the magazine to an early demise. A brilliant, romantic and unstable poet, his career somewhat resembles that of Byron, and of Ezra Pound. Like Byron, he was both lyric poet and bitter satirist who scorned the middle-class society of his time. But like Ezra Pound, he later turned against the radicalism of his youth and passionately espoused the Fascist cause in the Spanish Civil War. His poetry early attracted the praise of T. S. Eliot, so that his reputation quickly surpassed that of his friends on *Voorslag*. In the beginning, his influence on the young van der Post was great.

Over the years, however, the influence of William Plomer upon his lifelong friend has proved much more important. Plomer combined in himself the characteristics of Englishman and native South African, having been born in the back country of Northern Transvaal, but educated in England. His autobiography, accurately entitled *Double Lives,* not only tells the story of these early years, and of the *Voorslag* venture, but also realizes the conflicts and contradictions to which an inhabitant of two different countries and cultures is subjected. And Plomer's later periods of residence in other and even more different lands (which furnished material for his *Stories of Four Countries*) also set the pattern for van der Post's later adventures on four continents. If Campbell was the romantic inspiration of van der Post's youth, Plomer has been literary guide and friend throughout his life.

When van der Post met Plomer in Durban, the first issue of *Voorslag* had already been planned. (It was published in June, 1926.) The name, *Voorslag*, was the Afrikaans word for "whiplash," and had been chosen (as Plomer later explained) because "it was intended to sting with satire the mental hindquarters, so to speak, of the bovine citizenry of the Union."[7] The choice of an Afrikaans word also suggested the native African emphasis of the magazine. Yet the first issue was written in English, mostly by Campbell and Plomer, but including a philosophical essay by General Smuts.

Van der Post's first contribution to *Voorslag*,[8] written in Afrikaans, appeared in the second issue of the magazine. Entitled "*Kuns Ontwikkeling in Afrikaans,*" it proclaimed the development of Afrikaans as a cultural—rather than merely a political—language. (His father's two novels provided early examples.) His second contribution, "*Nimrods van die See,*" appeared in the third issue, and sketched the life of a South African whaling ship as the author had recently experienced it on two separate occasions. (Forty years later his fifth novel, *The Hunter and the Whale,* would convert these same youthful experiences into the form of imaginative literature.)

But the third issue of *Voorslag* also printed the formal resignations of the founding editors, and for all literary purposes marked the end of the magazine. A few undistinguished issues were written and published by other hands, intended to take the sting out of the old "whiplash." But the memory lingered on. Decades later a brand-new *Voorslag* would appear in Pretoria, published for more utilitarian purposes.

Meanwhile, the three young authors found themselves at loose ends. Although van der Post had kept his job on the *Advertiser,* he felt himself increasingly in disagreement with the editor. One afternoon an incident occurred which emphasized his conflict with all South African society. He had been playing with the Natal Hockey Team, of which he was captain, and, still in his hockey clothes, was having tea in a local restaurant when a loud altercation arose. The proprietor was refusing admittance to two Japanese reporters, because they were "coloured." Quickly van der Post insisted that they be allowed to enter, and to sit at his table as his guests. This chance meeting began a long chain of events which was to change the course both of his career and of William Plomer's, and which, sixteen years later, was to save his own life in the jungles of central Java during World War II.

It turned out that the Japanese reporters had been sent to Africa by their government to make contact with influential people, and to prepare the way for Japanese commerce and diplomacy—and, perhaps, for Japanese empire—in Africa. They had been brought by a Japanese vessel, now in Durban Harbor, and were authorized to bring back some important South African with them to visit Japan. The young man who had just now befriended them was an established journalist and a published author. He was free of commitments, he was eager to travel, and he was chosen for the invitation. After further conversations, he persuaded his hosts to include the eminent novelist, William Plomer. And so, taking leave of absence from his job on the *Advertiser*, he, with Plomer, sailed North from South Africa to see the world.

## VI  In A Province

When he returned to Durban a few months later, he had enjoyed many new experiences in foreign lands, many long talks with Plomer, and long periods of leisure at sea during which he could look back on his South African life and see it in perspective. He remembers: "I returned to South Africa to another year of rapidly growing differences not only with my newspaper but my own countrymen, started anew by another book of Plomer's, *I Speak of Africa,* which caused an even greater uproar than its predecessor." This year, 1927, was to be the first of several. Now, and repeatedly in the future, he was to wrestle with the fundamental problem of identity, or belonging: Where ought he to live? To what country did he owe allegiance? Where, ultimately, was "home"? Already he had realized that "Africa" was really two different countries or cultures: the South Africa of white supremacy and segregation, represented by his Grey College School and his *Natal Advertiser;* and the greater Africa of his childhood on an African Farm, where all the races had lived and worked together in mutual respect. He knew that in spirit he belonged to this greater Africa. But the actual country and government of South Africa, where his farm still physically existed, was increasingly rejecting this greater Africa of his memory and his hope.

During this year of growing conflicts with newspaper and countrymen, he met a young lady named Marjorie Wendt. Her father was founder and conductor of the Capetown Orchestra, her mother an English actress who considered South Africa a colony with little culture. She herself had been born in London. As the young couple fell in love, the idea of moving to London to live came to seem more and more attractive. His friend Roy Campbell had already returned to England with his wife, and William Plomer (who had stayed on in Japan) would later return there to live. Early in 1928 he resigned his job and sailed for London, to marry and to begin his career as a man of letters in the capital of the English-speaking world.

But a year and a half later, he found himself back in South Africa again. His friend Desmond Young, who had earlier reviewed *Voorslag* enthusiastically in his own newspaper, the *Natal Witness,* was now assistant managing editor of the *Cape Times,* and invited van der Post to join him as "leader writer." For fourteen months—through the year 1930—he remained in his old country and practiced his old profession. He remembers the date particularly, because it was the year of the death of D. H. Lawrence. On receiving news of the novelist's death via teletype one evening, he immediately wrote an enthusiastic obituary notice for the paper, and substituted it for the leading article which had already been set up—half expecting the editor to scold him for his presumption the next day. On the contrary, however, the editor was pleased that the paper should thus have identified itself with literature and culture.

But things did not always turn out so well. Desmond Young has described his own tribulations during these years in his autobiography, *Try Anything Twice,* where he states flatly that "the years I spent with the *Cape Times* were the unhappiest and the most frustrating I have ever known."[9] Of all the experiences contributing to this frustration, the most spectacular was the last. Since this final disaster was one in which he and van der Post shared equally, and since it typifies the conflict between the liberal journalists and their conservative countrymen of South Africa, it is worth repeating in detail.

One Sunday morning, [Young remembers] Laurens van der Post came to me with a startling story. Some Cape coloured prisoners, men and women, had been beaten up with gross brutality by the Dutch police in Caledon jail. Because he spoke perfect Afrikaans, he had managed to interview them and obtain their statements. He had also taken photographs of their injuries. It was a clear though by no means an uncommon case.

Together we wrote the story, with closest attention to the law of libel. When we published it on the main news page, it caused a sensation. There was a full-dress debate in the House of Assembly. Feelings ran high. Both Smuts and Herzog spoke at length. So precise and well documented were the allegations that the Nationalist Government had no option but to send the constables for trial. *The Cape Times* was freely quoted, praised and derided. But no one suggested that it had done more than report.

The result was inevitable. A Caledon jury acquitted all the ac-
cused. . . . [The managing editor then wrote an editorial.] Unfortunately, in criticizing the verdict, he said that the jury had *deliberately*
gone against the weight of the evidence. Reading the leader the next
morning, I sprang out of bed. "Good God," I exclaimed, "*The Cape
Times* is sunk!"

So it proved. The word "deliberately" was fatal. A man might make
a mistake; to suggest that he had done so "deliberately" was clearly
libelous. When the first juror brought an action and was awarded
heavy damages, with costs, the other eleven cases had to be settled
out of court. The affair cost the paper more than 10,000 pounds.

By now I was sick of *The Cape Times*. I also imagined, wrongly,
that I was sick of South Africa. Better go back to somewhere more
civilized.[10]

Unhappy and frustrated, the English journalist could then go
home, or "back to somewhere more civilized." But, even more
unhappy and frustrated, the native journalist could only leave
home again for European "civilization." Like the crusading, or
"muck-raking" journalists who had flourished in America in the
1920's, and who had done much to correct the abuses of power,
van der Post had documented the abuses. But in South Africa
such crusades could only result in failure, because a jury would
"inevitably" fail to convict. One might avoid the lawsuits and
the damages, if one weighed every word carefully. But if one
hoped to preserve one's sanity and to achieve perspective, one
must leave home again.

Back in Europe, he gradually succeeded in achieving perspective. The result was the writing of his first novel, *In A Province*.
Many of the events of this novel, including the vivid incidents
of racial strife and injustice, were derived from his periods of
reporting on the *Advertiser*, and the *Cape Times*. For instance
the "crime" of miscegenation between a black woman and a
white man, in which the black woman was found guilty by a
jury, but the white man was found innocent by the same jury,
suggests the same spirit of bitter frustration as that engendered
by the historic jury which had refused to convict of police brutality in the Caledon jail. But the novel now succeeded in setting
these painful events in perspective.

The title, *In A Province*, was derived from a verse of Ecclesi-
astes: "If thou seest the oppression of the poor, and the violent

perverting of judgment and justice in a province, marvel not at the matter." The verse and the title had been suggested by his friend William Plomer. But the Biblical source was one which he might well have chosen for himself, because the Bible had always provided him a deep sense of understanding, below the surface level of worldly wisdom. If the contemporary society of South Africa seemed hopelessly "provincial," when observed from the civilized capitals of Europe, it might prove only a local and temporal perversion of justice, which time and understanding might cure.

Even after he had returned to Europe, and after he had achieved the perspective reflected in his first novel, he still retained a deep sense of personal involvement in the Africa of his birth. Repeatedly during the 1930's he returned to Africa, spending "a great deal of time traveling between England and Africa, as well as walking and traveling all over Africa until the war broke out."[11] The long voyages between England and Africa (such as one described in *The Face Beside the Fire*), perhaps reflected his sense of aimlessness and frustration. But the long walks into the back country of Africa, to seek out some wise man of the Zulus, and to learn the myths of aboriginal Africa (as described in *The Dark Eye in Africa*), provided him with the knowledge and the understanding of that larger Africa which was to find expression in his best books after the war.

Finally, after discharge from the armed services at the end of World War II, and after his governmental appointment in the Far East, he returned to his native South Africa once again to make his home. For the third time in his life he accepted an appointment on a South African newspaper (the *Natal Daily News*), and held it for a full year. Knowing that racial relations had deteriorated and that government policy had moved even farther to the right, he still hoped to live in his native land. In order to return "home," he steeled himself to accept the conditions which existed there. But after the year which he had set himself, he finally gave up, because he could not write successfully under those conditions. Early in 1949 he returned to England to a new marriage and a new home.

Almost at once, however, he returned again to Africa on the first of a series of missions of exploration, in service of the British government (as described in *Venture to the Interior*). But now the center of gravity had shifted. Although Africa remained the source, the origin, the "interior," the center of perception and of judgment had shifted outside Africa. Besides his many expeditions of exploration to Nyasaland and the Kalahari, he continued to visit other parts of Africa and to speak and work for such organizations as "Capricorn." And he continued to visit South Africa frequently. As he published more and more books which freely criticized the racial policies of the South African government, and as those books attracted more and more readers from all the countries of the world, his relations with his native country became increasingly strained.

He still keeps his South African citizenship. He still visits the country every year or two. And he still directs the business operations of his ancestral farm. But, as he describes it, "my present relationship with the South African government is as bad as it could be." About 1960 he was put on a black list laid before the Parliament, of "people who have poisoned and corrupted opinion in the world against South Africa." None the less,

I go on speaking my mind whenever I am in South Africa. . . . On three major occasions [in 1964] I delivered stinging addresses in public against the system in South Africa. Not only were they fully reported in the press but also nothing was done to me. This is the extraordinary paradox of South Africa. I think one half of the country would like to shoot me and the other half, on the last occasion I was there, gave me a handsome literary award for *The Seed and the Sower*, and the University of Natal conferred a degree of Doctor of Literature on me.[12]

At this date of writing, he is planning a visit to South Africa again.

# CHAPTER 2

# *England, Indonesia, and the End of Empire*

## I  *From Durban to Kobe*

ON September 2, 1926, Laurens van der Post and William Plomer embarked on the *Canada Maru*, a Japanese cargo ship under the command of Katsué Mori, for the long voyage from Durban to Kobe. They were the only passengers at first, although a group of Japanese big-game hunters embarked when the ship touched at Mombasa, and throughout the voyage they were the only occidentals. Van der Post was nineteen years old at the time, yet had already been working as reporter for more than a year. And through his own initiative he had met the two Japanese reporters who, in turn, had obtained from Captain Mori the invitation to the two South African writers to visit Japan.

History had brought these Japanese to South Africa: Japan was in the midst of her process of industrialization, and was seeking new markets for her manufactured products. (Unfortunately, she had sold the South Africans a shipment of cheap pencils, each containing only one half inch of lead ten years earlier.) Further, Japan was now seeking to imitate the great European nations by establishing some imperial colony in Africa. (Abyssinia was the only significant part of Africa not yet preempted, and Japan had Abyssinia in mind.) Yet the Japanese were "*nouveaux riches*" and were sensitive to snubs from the established powers. (Captain Mori became furious when the governor of Kenya, whom he had entertained on the *Canada Maru* on his previous voyage, found it inconvenient to invite him during this voyage for a return visit in Nairobi.) And worst of all, the Japanese were members of the yellow race, who found themselves socially unacceptable to members of the white race, especially in South Africa, although they in turn looked

37

down upon members of the brown and black races. Seeking empire at the very time when empire was beginning to go out of fashion, and seeking to overcome race prejudice in the most segregated country of the world, these Japanese seemed doomed to defeat.

But if history had brought the Japanese to visit South Africa at this time, it was individual personality that enabled van der Post and Plomer to sail North and East to visit Japan at imperial invitation. "We were very young, it was true, and had no official status, but we had one quality very rare among white people in South Africa, a complete absence of racial prejudice."[1] This rare quality, which had already expressed itself in authorship and in action, now led van der Post to visit the Orient before he had visited Europe. Because he lacked the quality which has dominated the history of his native country, his life would embrace not only Africa and his ancestral Europe, but the Eastern continent of Asia as well.

This voyage introduced the two authors to other parts of Africa and of the East, before Japan. In *Venture to the Interior* van der Post recalled how he had visited Nairobi "for the first time twenty-three years before, with William Plomer and Katsué Mori." And Plomer has told of their incongruous adventures as young occidental guests of a Japanese sea captain in an East African country unaccustomed to the social mixing of the races. After Nairobi, they visited Singapore, as well.

But more important than any geographical adventures were their incidental experiences with their Japanese hosts on the small ship. Plomer remembers: "One night by the full moon a feast in Japanese style was held on deck, and much saké was drunk. One of the big-game boys sang some lachrymose love-songs in the style of a cat in rut, and van der Post and I obliged to the best of our ability with music-hall ditties and Afrikaans folk-songs.—*Vat jou goed en trek, Ferreira!* and so on. I also essayed a solo in Zulu. . . . Presently Mori, flushed with drink and in some *déshabillé*, performed with great vigour and technical skill what was obviously a war-dance; and looking at his clean and muscular feet one felt that he would like to plant them on the neck of a defeated enemy. For a few minutes the atmosphere was uncomfortable; equivocal looks and remarks were exchanged by the Japanese, and we knew without a doubt that he was dancing in honour of *der Tag*."² Sixteen years later van der Post would experience the Day then prophesied, when another group of Japanese seeking empire would capture and imprison him in another alien land.

The most important, although the least spectacular of his experiences on the *Canada Maru,* was the gradual learning of the Japanese language. During the voyage he and Plomer studied their dictionaries at the same time that they listened to their hosts talk with one another, and at times received helpful instruction as well. By the time they reached Japan they were able to ask polite questions in Japanese. During their intensive two-week visit they continued their education. And when Plomer decided to remain in Japan, van der Post would return without his friend, with none but Japanese to converse with on the long voyage home.

Meanwhile the highlight of the journey, of course, was the actual two weeks in Japan. On arrival in Kobe an active group of reporters and photographers welcomed them, and their visit was well publicized. As guests of the Japanese government, they received the red-carpet treatment. Not only did they visit all the famous tourist places, with trips to Nikko and Isé, to Kyoto and Nara; but they were entertained in a series of public and private ceremonies of all kinds. The redoubtable Captain Mori arranged a geisha party for his guests, personally selecting his favorite girls to entertain them. After drinking "enough saké to float a sampan," they slept late the next day, only to face another, more formal dinner party, given by the heads of the shipping company. When the *Canada Maru* finally set sail for South Africa two weeks later, van der Post had seen much of the world, even more of the Japanese, and had learned the Japanese manners and language. On the voyage home he would sort out the new experiences and impressions.

## II  *England and Authorship*

A little more than a year after his return from Japan, van der Post left Africa for England, early in 1928. Soon after his arrival there he married Marjorie Wendt, whom he had first met in South Africa. The couple settled in London, while he devoted himself to the profession of writing. In 1929 Jan Laurens van der

Post was born, the son's name reversing the given names of the father.

In 1929 also, his first article to be published in an English magazine was accepted by *The Realist*. "South Africa in the Melting Pot" appeared in the November issue, with the appended note that the author, who had done literary and journalistic work in South Africa, was, at that time, in South Africa. The article itself ended with the phophecy: "the future civilisation of South Africa is, I believe, neither white nor black, but brown. . . ."—thus continuing the theme first suggested by Plomer's novel, *Turbott Wolfe*, even while it cautiously emphasized that the prophecy could only be realized in the far distant future. Both the subject of the article, and the note concerning the author, underlined again his preoccupation with the problems of his native country.

During the next five years he continued to write for English magazines, while continuing to "commute" between England and South Africa. A few articles were published in the old *Nation and Athanaeum*. But other articles and short stories went unpublished, until—many years later—all were destroyed in the wartime bombing of London. For him, even more than for most young men, these were years of the great depression. From 1929 to 1934 he was attempting to make his home in an alien land, to make his living at a precarious profession, and to write literature in a foreign language, while young men everywhere were struggling against blind forces that they could not understand.

The positive results of these years were mostly intangible and future. He met many other apprentice writers and some established ones. (E. M. Forster would soon recommend the manuscript of *In A Province* to his publishers.) He continued to read widely, as he had always done. His favorite novelists included D. H. Lawrence, Conrad, and Thomas Mann. (Mann would later write praising his *Face Beside the Fire*.) He read widely in psychology and philosophy, preferring the seminal ideas of Carl Jung to the more "dogmatic" pronouncements of Freud. Meanwhile he occasionally reviewed current books for magazines and newspapers. (He had already reviewed the American poetry of Robinson Jeffers for the South African *Cape Times*.) But the results were scattering.

The one significant achievement of this period, which brought his literary powers to a focus, was the writing of his first novel, *In A Province*. In 1933 a friend lent him his villa in France, to which he happily retired, escaping all the problems and distractions of the London literary scene. There, while learning to speak another foreign language in another foreign land, he was able to look back at his own native land with all its problems, not only from new perspectives of time and place, but from the new security of temporary isolation. And he symbolized this temporary security and peace by the device of placing his South African hero, van Bredepoel, in a country town, where he is recovering from a mysterious illness.

Forwarded to England, this manuscript was read by his friend William Plomer (recently returned to England, after his years in the Orient), and others. In due time it was published by The Hogarth Press, which was to publish all his subsequent books. Considering the fact that this was the first book by a South African writer little known in England, the novel was well reviewed. Most enthusiastic, and most significant, was the essay-review by Stephen Spender, which was quickly republished in his book, *The Destructive Element: A Study of Modern Writers and Beliefs*. Significantly, the essay included two other novels, and was entitled: "Upward, Kafka and van der Post." It compared and contrasted *In A Province* with the Marxian story of Edward Upward and the typically symbolic novel of Kafka.

This comparison, suggested by Spender's essay-review, helps to explain many things. By focusing on the theme of social unrest common to these novels, and on the Communist exploitation of this unrest, it emphasizes the timeliness of *In A Province*. The novel not only deals with the racial problems of South Africa, but also with the destructive nature of the Communist exploitation of those problems. For the understanding of van der Post's own life at this time, and of his own psychological troubles, the comparison with Kafka also suggests the nature of his frustrations. Finally, by emphasizing that all Communist exploitation is destructive—not only on the level of actions, as described in the plot of van der Post's novel, but also on the level of literary and psychological truth, Spender suggested the quality of mind which would later enable van der Post to overcome his temporary frustrations and defeats. He concluded this essay with the key sentence of his book: "It is destructive for an artist to say

that he knows something which he only believes or hopes to
be true."[3]

In spite of van der Post's discouragement with the racial problems and repressions of South Africa, he did not oversimplify
them, or imply that there were any easy answers. And in spite
of his discouragement with the conditions and frustrations engendered by the great depression, he did not accept the over-
simplification of the Communist answer. *In A Province* remains
a totally honest work, which reflects clearly the desperate confusion of all its characters, including equally the Communist
agitator and the deeply disturbed autobiographical hero.

### III   *"The Growth of Nothing"*

The success of this first novel, and the excellence of its writing, should, logically, have opened the way to a brilliant career.
But biography and literary inspiration do not always follow
logic. After the success of *In A Province,* he published nothing
—and wrote nothing of importance—for seventeen years.

After the writing of his novel, but before its publication, he
bought a farm in the Cotswolds, Gloucestershire, and retired
from London literary life. His friends ascribed this move to his
"love of animals and the open air"; and the farm did allow him
to pursue his earliest vocation and to return to the good earth.
But retirement to the farm also gave expression to his growing
disillusionment with the conventional life of London, and with
the preoccupation of its Prufrocks with their coffee spoons. Like
his autobiographical hero, van Bredepoel, he retired to the
country and a life as close as possible to the life of his childhood, in order to recuperate from the discontents of civilization.
Like the earlier American idealists of Brook Farm, he believed
that he would be able to "farm with one hand and write with
the other." But even though he had been trained in the vocation
of farming far more effectively than those idealists, he found
that "the moment I got on the farm the farm took over and I
had no time or energy for writing because I was working and
milking cows every day from 4:30 A.M. to 9:30 P.M. Then the
war came. . . ."[4]

The physical reasons for the failure of the farmer to write fine
literature are obvious, and have often been demonstrated be-

fore. But the psychological reasons for the retirement of the successful writer to a farm, and for his persistence in living there for five years—after having proved to himself that he could not write there successfully—are more complex and obscure. The economic depression contributed, of course, but financial reasons were not compelling. Disillusion with an overcivilized literary life was more important, and the South African novelist shared with the American T. S. Eliot the inevitable homesickness of a foreigner in his adopted land. But the greatest element of disillusion was the vaguest—a kind of Kafkaesque quality of inner confusion, combined with an indefinable feeling of guilt and betrayal.

In *The Seed and the Sower,* van der Post characterized this universal element of psychological depression by the title, "the growth of nothing." And most of his novels have described the discouragements and disillusions of the young men of the depression era, in terms of different characters and circumstances. All are to some degree autobiographical, and suggest his own condition at this time.

Writing after the war, he remembers that at this time "most of my friends were communist." And his first novel, actually written at this time, centers upon the problems raised by Communist activity in South Africa. The physical and psychological sickness of its autobiographical hero is caused by the combination of two forces: his feeling of guilt at not having assisted a black friend to overcome the injustices of segregated life, and his disbelief in the Communist methods by which another friend seeks to overcome these injustices. In *A Province* suggests how difficult it was for any South African, who disagreed strongly with the segregationalist policies of his government, to avoid the seductions of communism. Yet van der Post, in spite of his deeply felt opposition to these policies, and in spite of the commitment of many of his friends to communism, always emphasized the evil of both extremes. His later novel, *Flamingo Feather* (1955), imagined for its hero a South African anthropologist who, single-handed, would save a native tribe from subversion by international communism.

But neither economic depression nor Communist subversion seems the fundamental cause of the young author's loss of the creative impulse. More fundamental was the cultural alienation

of the native South African, born to the wild beauty of its coun-
tryside and the challenge of its many races, but driven into exile
by complex forces beyond his control, and unable to identify
himself with the civilization of his adopted land or to domesti-
cate himself in his new home. The story of this deeper alienation
is told more symbolically in the first novel which he wrote
after the war.

*The Face Beside the Fire* (1953) seems the most autobiographical of all his novels, because its plot follows the life-story
of a young South African artist who flees from his native land
to make his career in England. Settled in London, he succeeds
brilliantly at first, and marries an aristocratic English girl; but he
soon suffers from domestic unhappiness and the loss of his creative impulse. Only after much wandering does he eventually find
happiness and success after a new marriage. These general events
follow the pattern of the author's life so closely that it is difficult
to realize how few of the specific details are autobiographical.

The basic conflict of *The Face Beside the Fire* is between the
African inspiration of his youth (the face of his sister beside
the campfire, seen while a lion roars), and the aristocratic intel-
lectualism of the English establishment:

"You will see how much he has already learnt after eighteen months
of civilisation with us," said [the English critic] in his best manner.
"Already we've taught him to think a bit before rushing into paint,
to pay more attention to the demands of significant form and the
abstraction of fundamental pattern and design.... But here"—he took
in a whole room of [African] canvases with a disdainful sweep of the
hand—"here, though there is no denying an uprush of a certain crude
power, it is all too naive, too naturalistic, to be interesting."[5]

Soon the young artist signalizes the frustration of his creative
impulse by painting a semi-abstract portrait of himself entitled
"The Exile." Only much later does he recover the creative impulse after a symbolic return to Africa.

These novels describe in different ways the growth of some
vague spiritual sickness in the hero. This sickness results from
his confusion and guilt over the racial unrest of South Africa,
from his feeling of alienation and exile in England, and from
the combination of economic with psychological depression. "I
was at my wit's end," the hero of *The Seed and the Sower* ex-

plains. But "At that moment the War came. . . . I felt the burden of meaninglessness which had been growing in me so alarmingly of late fall away, and the savour returned to my tongue."

## IV  *Commando*

The individual heroes of van der Post's novels realize in different ways some of the fundamental patterns of human experience which preceded—and, in a sense, caused—World War II. But the ancestral history of the author included fighting in many wars, and the outbreak of this war now set him free to follow this ancestral pattern. Moreover, by volunteering as a commando in England he accomplished what he had been unable to accomplish in peacetime: he returned to Africa not only in the flesh, but in the spirit also.

His old friend, Desmond Young, has recalled:

At the outbreak of the war he applied for a commission in the Rifle Brigade. The Rifle Brigade was still exclusive and all candidates were closely questioned by an R. B. colonel. "Have you any special reason for wishing to join the regiment," Laurie was asked, "any family connection with it, for example?" "In a way I have," replied Laurie. "My father was captured by the first battalion in the South African War and he always said that it was the best battalion in the British Army. They still send him a regimental Christmas card every year and he still has a cap badge they gave him." This explained why someone with so exotic a name as van der Post was wearing black buttons and (his father's) silver cap badge.[6]

If the "exotic" African name of van der Post seemed to unfit its bearer for the exclusive British Rifle Brigade, it fitted him the more perfectly for service in the Abyssinian campaign, and particularly for leadership of the camel train which would approach Abyssinia by way of the upper Nile and seek to persuade the wild tribesmen to revolt against their Italian overlords. Even though he had never been to Abyssinia or seen a camel, he fitted this assignment so perfectly that he later recalled detailed incidents of the campaign in two of his books. Desmond Young has also recalled a somewhat different version of the campaign:

Shortly afterwards, with three hundred camels laden with Maria

Theresa dollars and six sergeants from the Brigade of Guards, he was
making his way into Italian-occupied Abyssinia to assist in rousing
the tribesmen to revolt. It was a dangerous mission, for the Italians
knew what was afoot and searched diligently for the column from the
air. In consequence, it was never able to camp for more than one
night in the same place and had spent many months trekking through
some of the wildest country in the world.

In the process of trekking through this wild country, his column eventually met and skirmished with the enemy. This first
skirmish was also van der Post's first introduction to the shoot-
ing war, and the incident seems even more revealing than any
which he has retold in his books. After the machine-gun fire had
died down and his companions had begun talking about the
action, one of them turned to him and asked: "What was that
you were shouting when they first attacked? It sounded like
swearing, but I couldn't recognize any words." And he remembered that he had been swearing in Sesuto, the language of the
Basuto tribesmen whom he had known in his youth on his
father's farm. In this first moment of mortal danger he had instinctively reacted with words used by native African farm-
hands, rather than with any English or Afrikaans imprecations.
The combination of wild African country and the commando-
type warfare natural to it had opened a door of his mind long
closed by civilization and the routines of peace.

He has retold other incidents of the Abyssinian campaign in
his books: the evening conference with the Sudanese camel-
drivers, their acceptance of his appeal for support in spite of
hardship and beyond duty, the continued suffering of the camel
train and its gradual attrition, and the eventual appearance of
a strange airplane (piloted by the young South African who
later would pilot the commercial plane flying his "Venture to the
Interior"), which now brought fresh war supplies to make the
camel route unnecessary. He has told how little the Abyssinian
tribesmen cared to join in the British war of liberation against
the Italians, because to them one European conqueror seemed
much like another. But gradually the campaign moved toward
its successful conclusion, and, once again, Desmond Young has
reported a revealing incident, near its end.

Like van der Post, Young had left South Africa after the

trouble on the *Cape Times*, but he had moved to India, where the outbreak of war found him. From the East, he also had come to Abyssinia, and one evening he and a friend were reconnoitering near Addis Ababa.

After dark, in a narrow gorge, we were trying to negotiate the rocky bed of a river, the bridge across it having been blown. Hardly a good place to spend the night, and the corporal had warned us that the "patriots" were active in this area—and undiscriminating. It was, therefore, with some relief that, emerging from the river, we heard on the other side the unmistakable sound of British "other ranks" in conversation. I called out. "Wait a minute, sir, and I'll fetch the officer," replied a friendly voice. But the officer had already heard. "What on earth are you doing here, Desmond?" he said. "Come over and have a drink." This was Laurens van der Post, whom I had last seen when we worked on the *Cape Times* together, eleven years before.

The two South African friends met by chance in the Abyssinian wilderness in the middle of a world war, visited for a while, until Young had to leave. Half an hour after his departure (he would learn years later) van der Post's detachment had been attacked by tribesmen and again he had had to fight for his life. At the end of the Abyssinian campaign, van der Post was assigned to commando duty on the North African front. There he met David Stirling, to whom he later dedicated *The Dark Eye in Africa* (1955). In *The Dark Eye* he has told how Stirling organized some spectacular commando raids which traveled deep into the Sahara Desert to attack the German supply lines hundreds of miles from the front, and how on one of these Stirling was captured by the Germans, as van der Post would later be captured by the Japanese. But he has described a North African commando raid of the more conventional type in the central section of *The Seed and the Sower*. There, isolated from the spectacular individualism of Stirling's tactics and of his own career, the fictional description realizes the simple violence and horror of all commando warfare. The hero has surprised a sleeping enemy outpost, and is about to kill the dozing sentry with his knife. "In the midst of this stillness I heard his skin squeak at the point of my knife and then snap like elastic. A look like the brush of a crow's wing passed over his face." In North Africa the intimate violence of commando warfare found realization even more fully than it had earlier in the gun-fighting of the Ethiopian campaign.

Before the end of the North African campaign, however, van der Post was dispatched on a new, secret mission to Syria. Whether or not this actual mission resembled that imagined for the fictional hero of *The Seed and the Sower* (who is sent from North Africa to Palestine to found a school of commando war-fare on the very site of Christ's last meeting with his disciples), the geographical pattern of fact and fiction is much the same. The story of violence moves from Africa to the Near East, and finally to the Far East. And whether or not any actual experi-ence of van der Post's near the Holy Land contributed to any revulsion from the violence of commando warfare, and to any later experience of "conversion," the emotional progression from violence to revulsion to reconciliation was much the same in fact as in fiction.

When the Japanese attacked Pearl Harbor, van der Post was reassigned to Burma. While his ship was still at sea, the radio reported that Singapore had fallen, and he was diverted to Sumatra. But not for long. After the Japanese capture of Palem-bang, he withdrew to Java. There, after the collapse of all formal military resistance, he was assigned the almost hopeless task of organizing guerrilla resistance to the victorious Japanese.

The success of his earlier leadership of the expedition into Abyssinia had made him the logical choice for leadership of this last commando campaign. But the conditions had radically changed. Now the enemy controlled all lines of supply, by both sea and air, and his commandos must live off the land. Gradually they were worn down by wounds, disease, and hunger. Worst of all, they learned that the native peoples neither cared nor dared to help them. If the Abyssinian "patriots" had earlier failed to "discriminate" between the Italians and the British, the Indonesians, if anything, favored their Asiatic Japanese in-vaders. The dragon's teeth of conquest sown (although unknow-ingly) by the Dutch now sprouted hostility against all Euro-pean liberators.

For four months the guerrilla force held out, harassing the Japanese and moving from place to place. Then:

Early one morning I suddenly saw Japanese soldiers dropping out of the trees all around me. I had been betrayed by a deserting Chinese servant, and our small force had been surrounded by the Japanese during the night. A Japanese lieutenant shrieked an order, a platoon of Japanese fixed bayonets and charged straight at me, moving in a closing circle.

I held up my hand—and then, out of the irrelevant past, came a relevant word. There are many degrees of polite speech in Japanese. The politest form of all came unbidden to my tongue, although I had not spoken Japanese for sixteen years.

I called out a Japanese phrase which can only be translated idiomatically as: "Would you please be so kind as to condescend to wait an honorable moment?"

The advancing soldiers stopped dead. . . . Amazed, the officer walked up to me, pushed the point of his sword into my navel and asked: "Was that Japanese you spoke?"

And so my life was saved.[7]

## V  *Prisoner-of-War*

His life was saved because he had learned Japanese on a visit to Japan sixteen years before, and (much more remarkable) had remembered its most polite form of address in the midst of sudden emergency and disaster. His words had truly saved his life, because the Japanese were always loath to take prisoners, believing that all soldiers should fight to the death. Yet because the Japanese also believed that guerrilla troops who continued to resist after their commander had surrendered were disobedient to military law, his life remained in jeopardy. His captors threw him into solitary confinement and continued to question, threaten, and torture him. Writing *The Lost World of the Kalahari* fifteen years later, he would remember "the night I was thrown into a Japanese cell and the sentry with a grin assured me that my head would be cut off in the morning," as a turning point of his life. That night he dreamed of his childhood in Africa, and he awoke feeling that all would be well. But the ensuing years of his experience as prisoner of war were to be the most difficult of his life.

Although the life of a prisoner-of-war is never easy, prisoners of the Japanese were often subjected to tortures, both physical and mental, which were foreign both to European convention and understanding. Japan had never subscribed to the Geneva convention, which formally attempted to regulate the treatment of prisoners. But beyond convention, the Japanese saw life with a kind of Cyclopean singleness which excluded all foreign conventions and beliefs. Besides scorning all prisoners as cowards, and accusing all guerrilla leaders of wilful disobedience, they believed in compelling prisoners to work, and they believed in torture as a means of compulsion. Recognizing that van der Post could understand their language, and even something of their psychology, they treated him better than most. Like the Cyclops who promised Odysseus that he would be eaten last, they respected him even though he was a foreigner. As with Odysseus, his years of imprisonment developed into a kind of contest, in which he sought to win survival for himself and his fellow prisoners by means of understanding, and outwitting, his captors.

The first weeks of imprisonment were the worst. He has never described this period of interrogation and torture autobiographically, but has projected it upon two fictional heroes. In *A Bar of Shadow* the pseudonymous Englishman "John Lawrence" suffers at the hands of the Japanese, but (like his author) his earlier experience as "military attaché in Tokyo" helps him to understand them. And the South African hero of *The Seed and the Sower*, Celliers, wins the grudging admiration of the Japanese through his physical and moral courage. Both are tortured and subjected to the inquisition of the secret police, until at last they are released to their fellow prisoners more dead than alive.

More than any physical tortures, however, the psychological tortures devised by the Japanese were calculated to break down the morale, or "wilfulness," of their prisoners. Most effective were the public executions which, periodically, all prisoners were summoned to witness. Accompanied by the violent ritual of a military spectacle, these exhibitions seemed the hardest to bear both because of their savagery, and (more important) their calculated cruelty. One particularly terrible execution of this sort is retold in detail near the end of *Venture to the Interior*. There, at the climax of the author's venture to the heart of darkness, this dark memory returns to haunt him. And he can make his peace with its horror only by recalling it in detail in the midst of the beauty of the African wilderness.

After he had been released from solitary confinement to join his fellow prisoners, therefore, he recognized the need of devising countermeasures to improve their morale. Although he himself had suffered physical torture, he had been able to understand his enemy. And most important, he himself had suffered defeat long ago, when his Afrikaner people had been conquered by the British, and he had learned from bitter experience how to make the best of defeat. He was now chosen second in command of the camp, so that he could organize its activities from within, yet not be held officially accountable by his captors. As virtual leader of the camp, he again succeeded in transcending defeat, and he taught his fellow prisoners how. "If ever I did any good in life," he remembers, "I did it then."

First was the fundamental task of reorienting these prisoners of the Japanese. Most had never before experienced defeat, and now felt its natural bitterness and despair. But below this natural bitterness lurked the inevitable self-doubt of the soldier who has chosen captivity rather than death, and van der Post himself continued to suffer something of this self-doubt. The scorn of the Japanese captors for the cowardly enemy who had allowed themselves to be captured was the most difficult to bear. But even here lay the beginning of wisdom. By recognizing the Japanese psychology as fundamentally alien to the European mind, self-doubt and despair might be transcended. The first necessity was to understand the Japanese mind. And the first step to this end was the Japanese language.

Van der Post began his captivity with an estimate that the war might last for twelve years. This involved planning for a long struggle for survival—not only the survival of hardship, but also of dreary routine and inactivity. Therefore he organized a kind of cooperative language school. Japanese came first, but it was also important that all prisoners should contribute what they could, and this group came from many nations and spoke many languages. While van der Post gave lessons in Japanese and in his native Afrikaans, others taught other languages, both formally and informally. He himself learned a smattering of Russian, which would help him two decades later in his tour of "all the Russias," from a fellow prisoner. And of course Chinese and the languages of Indonesia were native to the location.

A fundamental difficulty was the lack of all basic materials. There were no books, and little paper. The central story of *The Seed and the Sower* purports to have been written upon rolls of folded toilet paper, later buried under the floor of a Japanese prison. The texts and vocabularies of the actual language school were thus inscribed on actual toilet paper. Van der Post composed a grammar of the Afrikaans language on this material, and other prisoners composed poems on it. After the war he sought to dig up a poem written by a friend, which had impressed him as particularly beautiful, but the place of its burial had been obliterated.

Meanwhile there were other activities, more practical, and much more dangerous. An American airman whose plane had been shot down in the Java Sea had been brought here, together with one of the first miniature transistor radios concealed upon his person. This radio, whose existence was kept concealed from all but a few, provided news from the outside world. When its parts gave out, another prisoner who had been forced to act as radio-technician by the Japanese managed to requisition duplicate parts to keep it functioning. Although the Japanese suspected its existence, it was always successfully concealed in a succession of hiding places. Once it was built into a wooden chair, upon which the Japanese officer searching for it was invited to sit. At another time it was built into the sole of a wooden shoe. Meanwhile it provided the source of a series of miraculously accurate "rumors," which were duly reported in a secret prison newsletter, also inscribed on toilet paper, and signed by the editor, "John Lawrence"—a reversal of "Laurens Jan." As time went on this letter reported that Germany had been conquered, and later that the Philippines had been recaptured, and finally that a new kind of bomb—an atomic bomb had been exploded over Japan.

As the war drew to its close and the Japanese situation became more and more desperate, the condition of their captives became more and more critical. Only the sudden ending of the war following the explosion of the second atomic bomb prevented what might have been total extinction. Meanwhile van der Post had laid plans for a possible outbreak by the prisoners, and for possible psychological countermeasures to prevent such a catastrophe. The self-sacrifice imagined by the hero of *The Seed and the Sower* may reflect one such possible plan. But the constant battle of wits, with its combination of psychological and practical plans for survival, continued to the end.

After the war's end, when all prisoners of the Japanese were posted for rehabilitation and many were found in dangerous condition, the prisoners of this camp proved so outstandingly well-adjusted that some even suggested that it was the rehabilitation officers who needed rehabilitation. In *A Bar of Shadow,* "John Lawrence" explains that the bitter and blind hatred of the enemy cast its imprisoning "bar of shadow" most darkly upon those who had never experienced the defeat and despair of imprisonment and torture. And certainly in practice van der Post's long campaign of outwitting the enemy by means of understanding him achieved success.

Since then many of his fellow prisoners have borne witness to the more intangible inspiration of his personal example. Writing twenty years after the event Captain W. T. H. Nichols concluded his description of his old friend and comrade: "Such a man in a P. O. W. camp is the equivalent of a host of angels, shedding light and strength upon all the sorts and conditions of men who make up the sad community. Many lives were saved, tragedies averted and souls rescued by his activities and ministrations."[8] And the Australian sergeant, Frank Foster, wrote: "If Christ ever comes back to earth, it will be in the form of Colonel van der Post. He saved our sanity and our lives."[9]

## VI  *From Djakarta to The Hague*

When the prisoners-of-war of the Japanese walked free after the surrender of their captors, they faced a world in flux. Military victory was secure, but the political situation seemed close to chaos: although the Japanese had been defeated, they had effectively loosened the bonds of the empires once held by their conquerors. Now the British army remained in Indonesia to keep the peace, and to try to bring order out of chaos. But it faced an almost hopeless situation. The Dutch had been utterly discredited, and the peoples of Indonesia demanded an end to empire.

No white man knew better than van der Post the temper of the native peoples, both African and Indonesian. For three years he had lived in Indonesia—four months among the natives attempting to organize guerrilla warfare, and two and a half years in a Javanese jail. Now he was appointed military and political adviser to the British Commander in Batavia—or Djakarta, as it

was soon to be renamed. He quickly persuaded Lord Mountbatten, "my imaginative Commander-in-Chief," that new measures were in order. Even though the Indonesians had not been
eager to help the British to fight against the victorious Japanese,
they had not been hostile, and now he hoped that they might
cooperate, if their former rulers would agree to an eventual end
of empire. He persuaded Lord Mountbatten to dispatch him to
London for consultation with the British Cabinet. And from
London the British Prime Minister sent him to The Hague to try
to persuade the Dutch to grant a kind of dominion status to
their former empire in the East.

He has told of this historic mission in the Introduction to the
1960 edition of *The Dark Eye in Africa.* "There was one moment
immediately after the Japanese surrender when the peoples of
Indonesia were ready to forget and forgive their past and enter
into a new relationship with their former rulers. . . . It was one
of those rare instances in history when great opportunities are
born: what one might call a 'moment of innocence' occurred."
And he has told of his belief that he might actually have persuaded the Dutch Cabinet to modify their rigid stand and to
make some compromise with the Indonesian "patriots"—soon to
become the Indonesian "rebels." But the British Vice-Chief of
Staff warned him then of probable failure, and eventually his
mission to his ancestral country did fail.

Of course he did not know this yet. After two weeks in
Europe he returned to Indonesia for two more years of military
service, both as official adviser to the British and as unofficial
mediator between the Allies and the Indonesians. As long as
the British army remained in Java, he acted as military adviser
to Lord Mountbatten's Commander-in-Chief. Then, after the
British pulled out and the rebel regime achieved power, he became adviser to the British Minister to Indonesia.

During these years the political relations between Europeans
and Indonesians deteriorated. As it became apparent that the
Dutch had no intention of granting independence to their former
East Indian empire, even in conditional terms or by gradual
degrees, the Indonesian resistance hardened. And as it became
apparent that van der Post's early mission to The Hague had
failed to achieve the mediation he hoped for, the Indonesians
became impatient of all European mediators. He continued his

efforts to bring about some understanding, but his contacts with the rebels became more and more difficult. If, as principal mediator between the opposing forces, he had been welcome at first, his later missions became increasingly dangerous as the situation deteriorated. The personal good will and understanding which he embodied became less acceptable as it became apparent that they would not be realized in political action.

In 1947, therefore, after more than seven years of continuous military service, he was finally granted discharge from the British army. After two and a half years of violent commando warfare, and two and a half years of painful incarceration, he had spent the last two years as a soldier seeking to make peace. The experiences of all these years had been bitter to bear, and he has described this bitterness in the Preface to *Venture to the Interior*. He has emphasized the sense of humiliation of the grim prisoner-of-war years in that autobiography; still, in one sense, the last two years spent as peacemaker were the most difficult. Even the prisoner belongs to the military community of his fellows and receives their friendship and appreciation as his reward. But the peacemaker who fails receives little appreciation or reward—unless perhaps from his own conscience, or God.

# CHAPTER 3

# *After the War, the World*

## I  *The Beginning of Something*

IN 1947, after his discharge from the army and final return to
England, van der Post was honored by citation as Commander of the Order of the British Empire. The citation had
been prepared before the end of the war, but had been with-
held when he had been reported missing and presumed dead.
Now, when it was formally published, it specifically praised his
"gallant and distinguished conduct in the field before 1942" but
did not mention his activities after. The physical heroism of the
warrior was honored, but the more distinguished moral heroism
of the prisoner-of-war and the peacemaker was ignored.

Yet he now believed that just this kind of heroism was most
important. During his years as prisoner-of-war he had thought
deeply about the problems of empire and racial domination. The
old empires held by Europe in Africa and Asia had realized a
necessary phase of history, but that phase was ending. The great
problem now was to achieve the peaceful emancipation of the
subjected peoples of Africa and Asia, and he had been working
for the last two years to bring this about. In Indonesia he had
failed. But his conversations with Churchill had given him the
greatest admiration for his prime minister, and he believed that
"Churchill emancipated the British Empire from within." Only
the India of Gandhi was Churchill's blind spot, and soon India
too would be freed. Yet the greatest problem of empire was not
so much political as moral. It involved the emancipation of the
former empires from the racial prejudice which the politics of
empire had so long nurtured. And that problem of emancipation
from prejudice centered upon Africa—particularly the South
Africa which England could no longer dominate.

In 1948 he decided to return to South Africa once again to live. After eight years' absence from the England which had been his adopted home, he hoped to find his true home again in his native land. He was convinced that Africa was the stage upon which the next act of the drama of history would be played, and he was first of all an actor. The war had unsettled the old ways, and South Africa might have changed with the times. After a year he sadly learned that "you can't go home again." Yet even if he could not make South Africa his "home," he had conceived the idea of helping to build a greater Africa which men of all races and nations might call home.

During the North African campaign, he had met and talked with the young Scotch commando, David Stirling. Both had subsequently spent years of captivity as prisoners-of-war, and in their different prisons had come to the same conclusions. After the war Stirling also had moved to Africa to start a business career of his own. But he was troubled by the same racial prejudice which had always troubled van der Post. Out of their conversations both during and after the war, the idea which was later to become the "Society of Capricorn" was born. Even if racial segregation seemed entrenched in South Africa, the immense area of tropical Africa north of the Tropic of Capricorn might perhaps be freed from the inherited tragic pattern. The old idea of a multiracial society, once realized in miniature on the African farm of his boyhood, where all races had lived in mutual respect and all had found a home, might conceivably be realized in the new nations of tropical Africa, even under the majority rule of the dark races, and in political terms.

The basic idea of "Capricorn" was little more than the ancient idea of the brotherhood of man applied to the political conditions of modern Africa. But in modern Africa the different races were living in conditions so little resembling brotherhood that the idea seemed even more impossibly utopian than usual. During the next seven years he would develop and articulate this idea in the discussions and essays which developed into *The Dark Eye in Africa,* and there he would emphasize the historic causes which made the idea so difficult of application—and yet so urgently needed—in Africa. But during these years he would also devote much practical energy to helping David Stirling realize the idea by means of the organization of "Capricorn." Although

this practical activity would come later, the imagination of it
helped to allay the disappointment and frustration of the last
year in South Africa.

In 1949 he returned to England to live. But he did not return
to his old home there. Even before the war he had realized that
his first marriage had become uncertain: he had often been
absent from home for long periods of travel in Africa, and the
tension of the depression and prewar years had been difficult
for everyone. His wife is reported to have felt that it was difficult to be married to all of Africa. Now, after eight years of
total separation brought about by the war, his first marriage
ended in divorce.

Before the war he had met the lady who was to become his
second wife, Ingaret Giffard. At that time she also had been
married. In her own name she had published a novel, *Sigh No
more, Ladies,* and had written a play which had been produced
at Wyndham's, *Because We Must.* During the war she also had
grown away from her early life, and had been divorced. Now
when van der Post returned to England, the two were married.
They settled in London in the house at 13 Cadogan Street,
where they still live. And "13," as he was to point out in *Venture
to the Interior,* was his lucky number: December 13 had been
the date of his birth, and he had been the thirteenth child in his
family. It seemed as though he had been born to thrive on ad-
versity. The defeat and captivity, the alienation and divorce
which would have meant bad luck to most men, would bring
good luck to him. His final failure to make a home in South
Africa and the divorce which ended his first marriage in England
now set him free to find his new home—in number thirteen.

## II  *Jung and Zurich*

*Venture to the Interior* was dedicated to "Ingaret Giffard, in
order to defeat the latest of many separations." The war and the
years following, and the separations involved, had caused inevitable problems. During the war Ingaret Giffard had sought to
gain understanding through consultations with a Jungian analyst.
Now when her husband left again for Africa, she decided to go
to Zurich to consult a new analyst in the community which had
grown up about the person of Dr. Carl Gustav Jung. And when

her husband returned from Africa, he joined her there. The third part of his *Venture*, entitled "Encounter with the Mountain," quoted Gerard Manley Hopkins: "O the mind, mind has mountains; cliffs of fall/Frightful, sheer, no-man-fathomed . . ." While the man of action had been exploring Mlanje, the black mountain of Nyasaland, his wife had been exploring the inward mountains of the mind.

Long before the war van der Post had become interested in Jungian psychology, but like many other creative artists he had earlier gained some of the same insights, described more objectively and systematically by Jung, in the course of his own personal experience. Through a childhood of painful adjustment to the defeat of his Afrikaner people, he had learned to understand some of the emotional problems of alienation. And through a lifetime of association with different races, and of participation in different cultures, he had developed some of these insights further. Now when he settled in Zurich among men and women of different nationalities who were seeking new self-understanding from Jung and his associates, he found himself strangely at home. During long conversations with the doctors and patients who were studying there, he exchanged personal experiences and discussed new ideas. Soon he became accepted wholeheartedly by the community, even though he lacked any official connection with it. And many of the friendships which he made at that time have continued undiminished to the present day.

Most remarkable was the friendship which developed then between van der Post and Jung himself. One quality of Dr. Jung's greatness was his unique capacity for friendship, to which many men of many types and nationalities have borne witness. He seemed able to understand, and even to share the personal problems and sorrows of all the diverse people whom he met. And if this ability naturally contributed to his skill as a professional analyst, it found expression equally in many friendships of a purely personal nature. Richard Wilhelm, the German scholar who translated the almost untranslatable "I Ching, or Book of Changes," bore witness to Jung's intuitive understanding for his own love for an alien culture. A prioress of a small convent in the Black Forest was grateful for his understanding of her lonely search for God. Now van der Post experienced

Jung's immediate sympathy for his own love for Africa. "Until I met Dr. Jung," he writes, "I had a great loneliness about Africa which I carried around with me, apparently unable to communicate my feeling of Africa to others. To my amazement, I found in him the first person who saw Africa as I saw it and its people, and the loneliness was gone for good."[1]

To other people, Jung's intuitive sympathy with their innermost feelings has seemed almost mystical. But van der Post found this fellow feeling based also upon actual experience. In 1925 Jung had traveled via Nairobi to Northern Uganda, where he had spent a month with a primitive African tribe. He had lived among them, and studied their myths and beliefs, as a psychologist. Then he had traveled north through the Sudan, where one day his party had met a roving, savage tribe. He has told (in his posthumous book, *Memories, Dreams, Reflections*[2]) how this tribe performed a wild dance by moonlight, and how he himself joined in its gyrations, brandishing his rhinoceros-hide whip instead of a spear. But when the dance threatened to get out of hand, he finally stopped it by haranguing the dancers in a mock-serious manner, so that they went home laughing. Now as Jung told van der Post of these experiences, and the South African told of his own childhood and later experiences among the savage tribes, the instinctive sympathy of these two civilized men with the unconscious feelings of an uncivilized people created an immediate bond. Their friendship continued unabated until Jung's death in 1961.

The close relationship which developed between van der Post and Dr. Jung and the many students who surrounded him in Zurich, exerted a profound and lasting effect. It stimulated van der Post's interest in the writings of Jung, so that he now read thoroughly many of the books which he had only known casually before, and it led him to develop many of his own insights and ideas in a more coherent pattern. It introduced him to many new friends and acquaintances, and it provided him with a physical audience and a clear focus. For Jung had then become so famous, and his followers had become so numerous, that an official "C. G. Jung Institute" had been formed, and a "Psychological Club of Zurich" had been organized. Both in theory and in practice van der Post profited by this new stimulus and association.

The practical effects of this ideal association were both immediate and long-lasting. The "Psychological Club," which had
been begun primarily to provide a forum for the exchange and
discussion of Jungian ideas and practices, now invited van der
Post to address it. A summary of his talk on "Personal Experiences of Primitive Africa" was published in *Aus dem Jahresbericht, Psychologischer Club, Zürich,* in November, 1951. This
marked his first appearance in print in more than fifteen years—
although it was practically synchronous with the publication of
*Venture to the Interior.* It also marked the first of many talks to
Psychological Clubs and other related organizations. Most important of these was the address delivered March 3, 1954, to
"Dr. Meier, Dr. Jung, Ladies and Gentlemen," which formed
the "Basis for Discussion" of *The Dark Eye in Africa.* On other
occasions he spoke in Zurich on related subjects, such as "About
the Bushmen in Africa" (March, 1955). And as his fame spread,
he addressed larger organizations such as the cultural festival
of Ascona, Switzerland. Many of these lectures first introduced
the material and ideas later developed more fully in his books,
but some suggested new and valuable ideas which have not
otherwise been published.

As Jung's fame grew, and as the doctors who had studied
under him in Zurich returned to their native lands to practice,
new Psychological Institutes and Clubs such as those first organized in Zurich grew up in many of the major cities of the
world. And as van der Post's own fame grew, following the
publication of five major books in five years (1951-55), he was
often invited to lecture throughout Europe and America. Usually he has combined these formal public lectures, to literary
and academic audiences, with other more informal talks to
Analytical Psychology Clubs in London, New York and other
cities. These talks have often been "taped," and sometimes published in different forms, and many are available in psychological libraries (although some, including two vivid reminiscences
of Dr. Jung, are not yet available to the general reader). The
associations which began in Zurich in the early 1950's have continued to the present, and have helped to introduce the author
to new audiences throughout the world.

The effect of his association with Jung and his followers was
not only practical, but also literary. Jung had been deeply inter-

ested in the psychological interpretation of literary myths, which
he described as symbolic expressions of archetypal racial experiences. His associates developed these interpretations even
further than he: C. Kerenyi interpreted the Greek myths as
expressions of unconscious patterns, and Erich Neumann interpreted the myths of Egypt and the Near East as expressions of
the childhood dreams of the race. Van der Post met and talked
with these men at this time, and they strengthened his interest
in the myths of Africa, suggesting new patterns for interpreting
them. His *Dark Eye* first used racial myths to suggest an understanding of African psychology; later, his *Heart of the Hunter*
(1961) focused on the myths of the aboriginal Bushmen.

Since the war, all of his writing and thinking has emphasized
the unconscious and symbolic processes of life, which Jung also
emphasized. His style has become much less realistic than that
of his early articles and novel. And his thinking has emphasized
the psychological motivation of action rather than the practical,
the symbolic interpretation of experience rather than the literal.
These literary interests and techniques were developed and
strengthened during his association with Jung, but they were
conceived much earlier.

*Venture to the Interior* was written before his meeting with
Jung in Zurich: both the title and the conception suggest a
literary derivation from novels such as Conrad's *Heart of Darkness*, rather than a psychological one. His novella, *A Bar of
Shadow* (published in 1952) explains the cruelty of the com-
mandant of the prisoner-of-war camp in terms of the unconscious beliefs of the Japanese, but was the direct result of his
own experiences and insights before and during the war. Van
der Post's friendship with Jung was profound, and his association with Jung's disciples fruitful, but his reading of Jung's books
merely strengthened the patterns of thought which he had
already developed from personal experience and from literary
sources.

## III   Venture to the Interior

*Venture to the Interior* was first published in America in 1951,
several months before its English publication in 1952. The author
wished to see it in print as soon as possible, because his mother
(whose story introduced "Part I: The Journey in Time") was

then in poor health. His American publisher succeeded in producing the book expeditiously, and his mother was able to read it at leisure, before her death in 1953. She was happy to read the ancestral story of her own mother's rescue from the Matabele during the Great Trek, and the story of her own long and victorious life. But more important, she was happy to read the story of her youngest son's victory over the "bitterness" and "sense of humiliation" which his experiences in the war had caused. For *Venture to the Interior* told, essentially, the story of this inner victory, achieved by exploring both the mountains of Africa and of the mind.

That a book which attempted to communicate so large and vague an experience in so unorthodox a manner should have been so completely successful, is astonishing. From its first publication the critics welcomed *Venture,* and many were able to describe clearly the complex purpose and pattern of the book. In the *New York Times,* Orville Prescott characterized it as: "Beautifully written and deeply moving—a journey into the interior of the human spirit as well as into the interior of a little-known region of Central Africa." And the *Atlantic Monthly* welcomed Colonel van der Post to "the select company of contemplative men of action—adventurers with a streak of mysticism, such as Lawrence of Arabia, Orde Wingate, and Saint-Exupéry. His beautifully composed book catches the spirit of a continent and imprints it on the reader's mind. It casts a beam of light, too, into the sources of the hate which is bedeviling the West from Suez to uttermost Asia." Although some disliked its "streak of mysticism," almost all appreciated the vivid narrative and recognized the relation implied—both historic and symbolic —between the interior of Africa and the heart of darkness in the mind of man.

The book was equally successful in England and throughout the Western world. It became the Book Society Choice and received the Amy Woolf Memorial Prize. Since then it has often been reprinted, both in paperback, and (recently) in the "Queen's Classics Series." It is now assigned reading in the British State (public) schools, where it is the only contemporary book in the company of traditional classics from Shakespeare to Hardy. In 1963 it was described and analyzed in a pamphlet by I. L. Baker, in a series of "Notes on Chosen Texts." For a time

it was also assigned to students in South African schools. Many
European countries echoed the chorus of approval, and the
author received personal letters from all over the world, con-
firming that the personal feelings which he described so vividly
in his *Venture* were common to all men during and after the
world war.

This book initiated a period of intense creative activity, which
saw the writing and publication of five major books in five
years. For the twelve years previous, his life had been crammed
with action and with suffering; now these experiences cried for
expression. After writing *Venture* he retired for a time to Zurich,
where his interest in literary symbolism and analytic psychology
introduced him to new associates and new ideas. One might
have expected this author to transform himself now from man
of action to man of letters—at least for the duration of this intensely creative period. But he did not. Repeatedly during these
five years, and for a significant part of each, he returned to
Africa as explorer and man of action. Repeatedly he acted out
new ventures to the interior in different places and in different patterns.

"Van is certainly one of those people who never let grass grow
under their feet," exclaimed Frank Debenham, the leader of the
first government expedition to the Kalahari Desert after the war,
which included van der Post. "In fact," he continued, "he hardly
ever stays long enough in one place for the grass to notice that
his feet are there."[3] Van der Post has written that "the spirit of
man is nomad" and throughout this period of greatest creative
activity and success, he continued a nomad, both in flesh and
in spirit.

The unique actualization of this ideal of the eternal explorer
within the body and spirit of one man is described by the scientific author of *Kalahari Sand* (1953). Frank Debenham, then
Professor Emeritus of geography at Cambridge University, had
led scientific expeditions throughout his life, including an earlier
one to the Kalahari in 1945. An Australian by birth, he had explored the burning deserts of Australia and the frozen wastes of
Antarctica, and had published many successful books both scientific and popular. Now he wrote:

Waiting for me at the hotel was the man whom I rather think will be the dominant figure in this book. Just once or twice in a lifetime one meets a man whom one recognises instantly and instinctively as "after one's own heart," as the phrase goes, and for whom one falls almost at first handshake, and continues to fall even when one discovers differences of outlook. Such was the man whom I will call Van, whom you may think of as First Lieutenant if you like, since that was his temporary status at the time, but for whom you will soon find other names, as I did. If I were the titular head of the Mission, it was Van who was the real head . . .[4]

Throughout the 1950 expedition described in *Kalahari Sand*, "Van" constantly reappears in many different roles. He organizes and plans the expedition; he designs a pavilion of mosquito netting which is strung between the parked lorries at night, and which is always covered by millions of bugs; he rides with the rear lorry in clouds of dust to make sure that no one strays; he doctors the Professor when he suffers from acute dysentery and guards him from lions when he goes off into the bushes at night; and he joins the Professor in talking to a group of African school children about life in the Far East. *Kalahari Sand* includes a great deal of vivid detail, both practical and scientific, which van der Post's own *Lost World of the Kalahari* omits. And it describes the imaginative author of the later book as the scientific leader of the 1950 expedition observed him.

It was Van's custom when we knew the route ahead to walk off after an early morning cup of tea and let us pick him up anything from two to six miles further on. These were obviously times of meditation for him, away from the bustle of the camp, but his thoughts were just as much on immediate practical plans for the day as on the flights of philosophy he loved to indulge in. It was on one of these forerunner walks that he mounted on an anthill and signalled back to us that he had reached what one can only call The Road, that is, the W.N.L.A. track from Francistown across to Maun.[5]

"Mounted on an anthill," beckoning his scientific friends to follow, he was also exploring the way that would lead into his own "lost world"—the world which had existed before civilization began.

He returned again to the Kalahari with government expeditions in 1951 and 1952. Professor Debenham has explained that the purpose of these expeditions was to explore the country for possible future economic development—much as van der Post had explained the purpose of his own official mission to Nyasaland, earlier, in his *Venture to the Interior*. But van der Post himself had known the Kalahari before this, as he had never known Nyasaland. In *Venture* he tells how his mother went off at the age of eighty to pioneer a vast tract of land on the edge of the Kalahari Desert, which his father had bought many years before. Now his own physical explorations of the Kalahari included visits to his mother's land, and also a symbolic return to the world of his own family's pioneer past. More than any others, these expeditions to the Kalahari were also "ventures to the interior."

The pattern of sudden alternation between strenuous physical activity and writing, illustrated by these repeated explorations of the African back country during the same years that he was writing and publishing five of his best books, is a pattern repeated by the books themselves. He points out that all his books have alternated between "extrovert" and "introvert"—between stories emphasizing external action and adventure, and stories emphasizing inner feeling and hidden motive. *Venture*, for instance, in spite of its psychological overtones, had told the story of an actual journey, "in time" and "in space." Now *The Face Beside the Fire* told the stranger story of an artist's inward journey toward self-discovery and self-realization.

This second novel was published in 1953—the same year that his mother died. It described the life of a South African artist whose parents and childhood closely resembled the author's. But instead of the sharp historical narration of *Venture*, *The Face* now told its story more by symbol and by indirection. The book received somewhat mixed reviews: some praised its intensity and depth of insight, but others objected to its inwardness. A letter of praise from Thomas Mann emphasized its excellence and suggested its individual quality.

Meanwhile, *A Bar of Shadow* had appeared in *The Cornhill* magazine in 1952. Hardly more than a long short story, or (as some believed) an autobiographical narrative describing the author's actual experience in a Japanese prison camp, this little work produced a remarkably powerful effect. Some readers believed that it offered the best explanation of Japanese wartime psychology ever written. All praised its vivid description of the life of a Japanese prison camp. Two years after its first magazine publication, his English publishers issued this forty-page story as a separate book; two years later, his American publishers followed suit. It was soon translated into many foreign languages; one American reader first heard of van der Post when he picked up a German translation of this book in Tokyo and read it enthusiastically. The publication of so slim a volume in so many languages gave evidence of the rapidly growing fame of the author throughout the world.

## IV  *Africa and the Dark Eye*

During the postwar years van der Post was constantly active in the fields of journalism, exploration, and literary creation. His own books have described these activities, and some of his friends have described them in their books and memoirs. During these years he was also active in the field of public affairs. Yet neither he nor his friends have written much about this. The first edition of *The Dark Eye in Africa* appeared in 1955, with a dedication "To David Stirling, for practising what he preaches in Africa, and to those of all races and colours who are trying to make Capricorn a true instrument of reintegration in Africa." But the book included little description of Capricorn or its practices. Only when it was re-issued in 1960 did the author add a new Introduction to describe Capricorn for non-African readers, and to promise a future book about the organization "which David Stirling is about to write." However, Stirling's book has not yet appeared. In the field of politics—usually the most public of all human activities—van der Post's practical activities still remain obscure.

In due time more will probably be published about the activities of Capricorn and its founders. Yet the impression persists that van der Post is not a political person. Although he has constantly reaffirmed his personal dedication to the task of "changing the fatal pattern in Africa," he has left the task of political opposition to others, such as Alan Paton. In part, he believes that the fatal pattern can best be changed by educational activities devoted to molding public opinion—especially in the emerging nations north of Capricorn. But fundamentally, he himself thinks and acts in terms of individual personality rather than public organization. His personal friendship with Stirling is typical.

LIBRARY
**WAYNE STATE COLLEGE**
Wayne, Nebraska

During the postwar years, therefore, he joined Stirling in "formulating the basic principles on which a new society free of race, colour and religious discrimination could be set up and safeguarded." And his most effective political activity consisted in discussing these principles with African leaders and in lecturing about them to African audiences. The *Cape Times* reported (about 1960) that "he has toured British Africa and spoken with African speakers on a common theme side by side on the same platform in Kenya, Tanganyika, Nyasaland, Rhodesia and in the heart of the copper belt as well. He was, with David Stirling, the first European to do so, in days when it was not without danger."[6] At his best in private discussion and public lecture, he has lived to see his activities bear fruit in "the happy issue of events in Tanganyika," and in many other new African nations.

The remarkable fact about *The Dark Eye in Africa* is the comparative absence of political and economic facts and arguments. The immediate occasion and the ultimate purpose of the book were both psychological. It began as a lecture addressed to the C. G. Jung Institute and the Psychological Club of Zurich, in March, 1954. This lecture was repeated later to other Psychological Clubs in other cities. Its subtitle was "A Talk on the Invisible Origins of African Unrest," and its fundamental thesis was, precisely, that the true origins of racial unrest in Africa were psychological and "invisible," rather than economic and visible. "The Dark Eye" of the title was the only visible symbol and expression of the inner sense of outrage, engendered by the white man's scorn of the colored races rather than by his economic oppression of them. The book developed and took its form in the process of the author's answering a series of questions and objections to this basic thesis. Historical facts, such as the Zulu Wars, and economic facts, such as the higher standard of living resulting from the white man's rule, were adduced as counter-arguments by tradition-minded members of the audiences, only to be answered and rejected by the author-speaker. One can hardly imagine a less likely origin and formulation for a successful book.

*The Dark Eye* was published in 1955, both in England and in America. But in America the order of "The Discussion" (the dialogue of "Questions" and "Answers" which constitutes the bulk of the book) was altered, to make the author's discussion of "the

American angle" end the American edition. In a way, this altera-
tion was prophetic, for as the author admitted, "I have never
been to America," yet he was to visit America the next year. But
the English edition ended symbolically, as the author had intended, with the legend of the mythical white queen of Africa,
who had existed in the imaginations of black and white Africans
alike, and who had appeared in the aboriginal rock paintings of
the Kalahari, as well as in the self-conscious modern romances
of Rider Haggard. This African legend naturally suggested both
a psychological resolution to the argument and an artistic conclusion to the book.

Both in Europe and in America *The Dark Eye* was well reviewed. "If you fail to read it, you will miss one of the most
fascinating and profound statements to come out of Africa on
the subject of man's bitter war against himself," said the *New
York Times*. And Lillian Smith, herself an authority on the racial
question in America, repeated the praise: "This book about the
black man and the white man in Africa is the most important
and to me the most interesting that has been written on this fascinating subject." The psychological interpretation of the racial
conflict in terms of "man's bitter war against himself" raised the
African problem to universal dimensions, and fascinated readers
throughout the world. In spite of the awkwardness imposed by
the lecture-room origins of the book, and by its question-and-
answer development, it succeeded because of its personal immediacy and psychological depth.

This same year saw the publication of the author's most popular novel, *Flamingo Feather*. Frankly an adventure "yarn," the
book told a fast-moving tale of intrigue and exploration. Full of
the vivid detail of observed African landscapes, this novel was
concrete and "extrovert," where *The Dark Eye* was more abstract
and "introvert." "*Flamingo Feather* is that rarest of birds, a true
African novel of adventure, and a scintillating one at that," said
the *New York Times*. But *Flamingo Feather* also imagined, somewhat prophetically, the dangers of the Communist subversion of
a primitive African tribe, and thus emphasized important political issues. Its hero finally triumphed (significantly) not merely
by means of courage and skill, but by his deep understanding of
native psychology. The novel appealed to readers throughout the
free world and became the choice of the German Book Society.

Both *The Dark Eye* and *Flamingo Feather* reflected the author's continuing fascination with his native Africa and his increasing skill in communicating this. Both added to the reputation which his *Venture to the Interior* had already established, and which seemed to constitute him literary spokesman for Africa to the Western world. Before these books were published in 1955, he had been commissioned to write a long article on Africa for the American magazine *Holiday*, which had appeared in the March, 1954 issue. Brilliantly successful, this prepared the way for later *Holiday* articles on Japan (October, 1961), and the series on Russia, which later developed into the book of 1964.

Africa, however, remained his central theme. In 1964 he wrote a second long essay on Africa to serve as Introduction to the handsome volume of pictures of *The Nile* by the American photographer, Eliot Elisofon. Both these articles on Africa repeat the pattern established by *Venture* and emphasize the depth of his involvement with the dark continent, and the symbolic nature of it. The *Holiday* article of 1954 began with the author's remembrance of Africa in a Japanese prison during the war ("until then, I had no idea how much Africa meant to me") and continued to explain how Africa came to seem the very symbol of freedom, "a vast continent not yet imprisoned by the mind of man." Similarly, his Introduction to *The Nile* becomes (to a lesser degree) the personal interpretation of a symbolic experience. Beginning on the equator in the Ruwenzori range of "the Mountains of the Moon," the Nile begins to flow northward from the heart of darkness into the light of modern history. "In it alone myth and legend, the dream speculation of our first recorded histories, the gossip of centuries, and the sober facts that surround the life of the river, meet and are resolved." Although these articles sometimes repeat the details of experience and idea which *Venture* and *The Dark Eye* first related, they develop effectively the greater myth of an aboriginal Africa which had been growing in the depths of the author's mind and imagination.

## V  *Beyond Africa*

The same year, 1955, which saw the publication of *Flamingo Feather* and *The Dark Eye*, also saw the author's private expedition to the Kalahari, which was to become the subject of his next two books. He had, of course, already explored the Kalahari with three government expeditions, and had met and talked with different Bushman groups who inhabited the desert. Now he organized his own expedition in order to film these Bushmen for the British Broadcasting Company, and in addition to seek out the wildest Bushmen who lived farthest from civilization and record their oldest myths and dances. By means of this expedition (and the resulting motion pictures and books) he also hoped to arouse public opinion to the need of establishing new regulations and laws to protect the aboriginal Bushman race from extinction by the forces of civilization—those very economic forces which had motivated the earlier governmental expeditions to the Kalahari. In all these purposes he succeeded. The moving pictures taken then and released by the B.B.C. in 1956 were greeted with public enthusiasm. Ten years later they were shown on American television at exactly the same time that the author was lecturing to a University of California audience, so that he then found himself competing with his own earlier self.

The fundamental purpose of the 1955 expedition to the Kalahari, however, was not public and practical so much as private and personal, as the early chapters of his book would emphasize. Now he was seeking to explore not so much the actual Kalahari with its modern inhabitants, as the lost world of the remembered Bushmen of his childhood and the prehistoric world of the nomadic hunters in the childhood of the human race. Already he had explored the economically habitable part of the Kalahari—now he would explore its uninhabitable wasteland. And in this deepest interior he found the last remnants of a race who had miraculously kept themselves free, both from the white man's civilization and from the agricultural life of the black man as well.

This was his last organized venture into the African interior. It was also, symbolically, his venture into the last interior—into the innermost heart of the dark continent. It was his exploration of the archaic origins of African history, and of human history— as though the author were now pacing backward down the steps of man's earliest journey toward civilization, to discover an innermost desert blasted with excess of light. But then, having discovered the bright desert at the center of the heart of darkness, like Dante he seemed to reverse direction and to climb upward. Having explored the lost world of the Kalahari, he had

symbolically freed himself from bondage to his African childhood, in order to become a citizen of the larger world.

Returning to civilization, he edited the Kalahari film and began
work on his new book. But *The Lost World of the Kalahari* did
not write itself as easily as *Venture,* and he spent much time
seeking to organize his impressions of the Bushmen and their
myths. Because his fame was growing, he was invited to lecture
more frequently, and he often spoke of his recent experiences in
Africa. Most important was a two-hour talk given in August,
1956, to the festival at Ascona, on "The Creative Pattern in Primitive Africa," later published in the *Eranos Jahrbuch.* This
speech, like many delivered at this time and later, described
some of the experiences and myths later incorporated in his
books, but used them in different patterns.

His exploration of the life and myths of primitive Africa now
gave place to travels to new countries and to the New World.
Although *Venture* had first been published in America, and the
American magazine *Holiday* had commissioned his first and most
popular article on Africa (and later articles to come), he had
never visited America. In December, 1956, he landed in New
York to deliver a series of lectures; and on this occasion (as
often later), he emphasized the parallels between the peoples
of America and South Africa, especially in their common experience of having been transplanted from Europe into a primitive
new country. And he introduced himself to his first American
audience "as one who is perhaps more de-tribalized than most."[7]
In other talks during later visits to America he developed the
parallel between the two countries more fully:

I've always had a feeling that people like myself who were born in
Africa, ought to be able to talk to you who are of America in a way
in which perhaps no other two peoples in the world can talk, because
we both come from transplanted European communities. We both
were transplanted into continents which were comparatively primitive, and what is more, in addition to your own indigenous continent,
you, through your history, added to it a very large human content
coming from Africa. Therefore, perhaps what we can say to one
another is more meaningful than what any other peoples in the world
can say. Certainly I have always felt that we in Africa couldn't get
by without your help and, in a sense, without your example.[8]

In the course of these American visits, he has often participated in discussion groups and seminars dealing with the racial problems common to America and to Africa, and has sometimes been discouraged by the bitterness of Negro spokesmen—despite the progress being made in America, as contrasted with South Africa. He has repeatedly emphasized the need of "not letting ourselves be corrupted by what has hurt us," but also he has often been encouraged, and has added:

This can be done. I saw a wonderful example of it lived out in New York the other day. It is a little parable that I shall carry back with me to my own country.

I was in a taxi, and I noticed that my taxi was behaving in a very peculiar manner. Of course, taxis all over the world behave in a peculiar manner, but this was more peculiar than normal. And then I realized that my taxi, which was driven by a European, was racing another taxi; and, when the light turned red, he pulled up very close to it. Then I saw that the other taxi was driven by a negro. I hadn't noticed it, but obviously this man had cut in front of my taxi, and my driver was swearing, and cursing the chauffeur of the other taxi. The other driver tried to explain to my driver what had gone wrong, but he wouldn't listen at all.

Suddenly I saw an extraordinary expression come over the colored man's face. All at once he accepted responsibility for the situation; he took this anger and rage as something which the white man couldn't help. And he took out a package of cigarettes and he said, "Gee, I'm sorry. I've put you in wrong with yourself. Would it help you to get out of it if I gave you a package of cigarettes?"

And my driver instantly altered. He became a completely different man. "God almighty," he said, "I guess I've shot my mouth off too much!" To my amazement he shot away, nearly knocking the traffic sideways; he was so anxious to get away from the situation.

But there is the parable: if you accept your neighbor's heresy, his failing, as part of your own, you can both snap out of it.[9]

This fragment of American experience, translated easily into a parable of universal experience, may illustrate the larger pattern of the travels of this author throughout the world. Besides frequent visits to the United States and Canada, he has lectured through Europe from Spain to Scandinavia. Between these tours he has sometimes retired briefly to France or Italy to work on his books in quiet. If we add to these private travels his professional tours through Japan and Russia to gather materials for articles for *Holiday* magazine, we have the physical life of the spiritual nomad of the modern world. No longer exploring the wastelands of the Kalahari, he now travels through "The Waste Land" of modern civilization. But he enjoys our modern world wholeheartedly and finds its wastelands as fascinating as those of the African interior.

In 1958 *The Lost World of the Kalahari* was published, and received much the same enthusiastic reviews that had greeted *Venture* and *The Dark Eye*. Fellow authors and critics alike praised his descriptions and interpretations of Africa. Mary Renault, fellow countryman and author of *The King Must Die*, bore witness that: "Laurens van der Post's wisdom of the world is rare in its vivid insight and delicate compassion. In my view no other writer on the African scene can hold a candle to him." This latest book confirmed his earlier reputation as eloquent spokesman of modern Africa, and wise interpreter of its troubled spirit.

*The Heart of the Hunter,* published three years later, received mixed reviews. Its Introduction suggests why: "This book is a continuation of the story begun in *The Lost World of the Kalahari,* but can be read as a self-contained tale." Like all sequels, this suffered from lack of unity and continuity. Moreover it seemed to tell two separate stories: "Part One—World Lost" narrated the story of the physical conclusion of the author's earlier expedition to the Kalahari; while "Part Three—World Regained" described and interpreted the primitive myths which he had collected on that earlier journey. The book therefore lacked the excitement which the earlier story of the physical journey had communicated. And although the description of the Bushman myths included in "Part Three" was imaginative and moving, the subject matter limited its appeal to the larger public. Many found *The Heart of the Hunter* inferior to his earlier books, although some welcomed it as one of his best.

## VI   *East Is West*

In 1961 van der Post returned to the Far East, both in fact and in spirit. His second long article for *Holiday* (October, 1961) described an extensive tour of Japan which the American magazine had recently arranged for him. But this article became far more than the conventional travelogue and developed into a many-dimensional narrative, contrasting present impressions with past memories. It recalled both his first visit to Japan in 1926 and his later experiences with the Japanese during the war.

As he lands at the modern Tokyo airport, he remembers the first excitement of his arrival on the *Canada Maru* thirty-five years before, and the strangeness of the impact of an alien civilization on the mind of a young man. In the new Japan he observes the incongruous mixture of the traditional Oriental culture with the modern Western civilization superimposed upon it. But between the first memory of the traditional Orient and the recent experience of a cosmopolitan culture stands the unreconciled suffering of the war. For the first time he tells in detail the story of his capture by the Japanese in 1942 and his speech to the enemy commander in politest Japanese, which saved his life. Now, although some residue of the old bitterness remains, it is transformed by the memory of past hospitality and the experience of present hospitality, and by the understanding of the years between.

The same familiarity with Japanese language and culture, which had served him so well during the war, unlocks the door to many new experiences in Japan. He not only visits friends from the past but is able to travel to many places out of reach of Europeans who cannot speak the language. Traveling on Japanese buses and sleeping in Japanese-style lodgings, he visits remote regions of the empire. The primitive fishermen of the Northern island seem especially interesting in their resemblance to the primitive tribesmen whom he has known in Africa. And then, returning to the cosmopolitan civilization of the main island, he is suddenly struck by the "ugliness" of the white, European faces which, for the first time in several weeks, he sees again. Having immersed himself in Japanese culture and identified himself with the Japanese people he is even able to share their distaste for foreign faces. Before he leaves he finds himself in several situations mediating between the Japanese and other foreigners. This article, written by a South African journalist for an American magazine to describe travel in modern Japan, which began as journalism, becomes the autobiography of a citizen of both worlds.

Meanwhile, his struggle to reconcile himself to the memory of Japanese cruelty during the war had resulted in the writing of

several stories and fables. The autobiographical *Bar of Shadow*
had first appeared in 1952. Later he had imagined the fable of
a South African officer imprisoned by the Japanese, who had
been able to transcend his own bitterness, and finally, to sacrifice
himself in such a way that both his fellow prisoners, and ultimately even his jailors, were freed from the "bar of shadow," or
imprisoning hatred of the war. Now he developed and rewrote
this fable, added to it another story of wartime suffering, and
combined these with the original *A Bar of Shadow* to create a
new fictional "trilogy" about the war, called *The Seed and
the Sower.*

*The Seed and the Sower* was published in 1963. But in spite
of the fact that it included a story that had succeeded brilliantly
ten years before, and a second long story of great imaginative
power, the new book was poorly reviewed. The *New York Times,*
which had praised his earlier books, ignored this one. The *New
York Herald Tribune* reviewer thought that the stories bore evidence of an unresolved conflict within the mind of the author.
But other reviewers praised the book with superlatives, and the
University of Natal cited it first in awarding the author an hon-
orary degree. These extreme and opposite reactions suggest both
the unique quality of the book and its significance to the life of
its author. The inscrutable enemy had been understood, but the
self-sacrifice of the fictional hero seemed ambivalent to some.

Meanwhile the earlier articles on Africa and on Japan published in *Holiday* had proved so successful that the magazine
commissioned him to undertake a series of journeys through
Russia in order to write a series of articles on his experiences
there. He had always wanted to visit the only great country of
the world which stretched across both Europe and Asia, and
which seemed to belong to both worlds. Although he had always
admired its authors and artists, from his early years, even when
some of his friends had become Communists during the depression, he had been repelled by doctrinaire communism. During
the war he had met a Javanese rebel who had been trained for
twenty years in a school for world revolution near Tashkent.
Also, he had learned some Russian in the language school which
he had organized in his prisoner-of-war camp in Java. Now, after
many preliminary difficulties, he finally secured permission to
visit Russia.

When the articles about Russia which appeared in *Holiday* magazine were collected for publication in book form, they were given different titles in England and America. The English title, *Journey Into Russia*, suggested something of the spirit of *Venture to the Interior*, whereas the American one, *A View of All the Russias*, suggested rather the multiplicity of the cultures which still exist under the political unity of Soviet communism. This multiplicity was further emphasized by the mechanical difficulties imposed by the Russian "Intourist," which required that he break up his trip into four separate journeys, each starting afresh from Moscow. Therefore he first flew to Tashkent and Southern Russia, then took the train into Siberia as far as Lake Baikal, then returned to Moscow to fly direct to Khabarovsk, in the Russian Far East. His book vividly describes all these journeys. But one incident in the third journey illuminates the whole book.

Throughout Siberia he had been impressed by the spirit of enterprise animating the "pioneers" of this newly developed land —a spirit resembling that of the early pioneers of the American West. Now in Khabarovsk, in the Russian Far East, he was taken by a friend to the Ussuri River, which flows southwestward from Khabarovsk into China. But the Russian friend stopped short of the Chinese border, warning: "I don't think we had better go any farther." Then suddenly he began declaiming in deliberate English: "East is East, and West is West, and never the twain shall meet." Standing in farthest Siberia to the East of China, looking Westward toward the Chinese border, this Russian—like many Siberian pioneers—seemed to identify himself wholly with the "West." Somehow the established poles of the civilized world had become reversed. East was West and West was East, but the modern Russian echoed the old English poet of empire: "never the twain shall meet."

Published in 1964, this book on Russia was immediately successful. Although the author prefaced it with the disclaimer "I am not an expert on Russia," his observations seemed so vivid and his interpretations so illuminating that they appealed to all types of readers. Brooks Atkinson, columnist for the *New York Times* and himself a veteran of three professional tours of Russia, thought it the best book on the subject which he had read. The concrete personal experiences and the intimate conversations with individual Russians gave it first-hand reality, while its em-

phasis on the rigid mask imposed on the creative individual by
the Communist state explained why most Soviet writers feared
to express their feelings in conversation or in writing. At book's
end, van der Post tells how he was impressed by the beauty of
the free English faces he saw on leaving the country, as contrasted with the constrained masks of the Russian faces. But in
Japan he had been impressed by the seeming ugliness of the
European faces he had first seen on emerging from that country.

*Journey Into Russia* completed a cycle in the author's life.
Beginning in youth he had progressively visited most of the
countries of the world, spending years of his life in each of the
continents of Africa, Europe, and Asia. He had always enjoyed
travel, especially personal contacts with individuals in the foreign countries. He had always been able to feel at home with
people of different races and cultures, and to feel that he would
like to return to each. In Russia he enjoyed his conversations
with many private individuals—especially the artists and writers.
But, he says, he will never return to Soviet Russia. A quasi-
Oriental dictatorship of the spirit still denies freedom to the
creative individual.

In the course of his many travels he has become, literally,
reoriented. The geographical East no longer seems necessarily
"East," nor the West "West." Japan has become part Western in
spirit, and the disoriented Russian looking Westward into China
also imagined himself to belong to the "West"—and, relative to
Communist China, he may have been right. Van der Post has
not only visited most of the countries of the world, but his writing, like his life, has consisted of a series of journeys of discovery
into a series of strange lands and cultures. A citizen of the one
country where politically he feels least at home, and a resident
of another country to which he belongs neither by birth nor
nationality nor language, he has progressively become a citizen
of the larger world.

# PART TWO: THE BOOKS

## CHAPTER 4

# *Non-Fiction: "The Immense Journey"*

OF the ten books which Laurens van der Post has published, five are novels and five "non-fiction." His first book, *In A Province,* was a novel, but the book which made him famous, *Venture to the Interior,* was not. His most distinctive and successful books have belonged to that vague category called "non-fiction." Unique blends of autobiographical experience and imaginative insight, they have cut across the established boundaries of literary form to create new forms of their own. Rather than discuss his ten published books in chronological order, I shall try to define these "non-fictions" first.

Typically, *Venture to the Interior* begins with autobiography, then returns to describe the ancestral sources of this autobiographical life, using both autobiography and history to explore the paths of experience which have led to the present and whose interweaving patterns give it meaning. On the one hand, these books of non-fiction describe fragments of the autobiography which the earlier chapters of this book have narrated in chronological order. On the other hand, they suggest the patterns of feeling and idea which transcend individual experience and history.

All these books of non-fiction (except *The Dark Eye*) follow the pattern of "the long journey." Like the earliest myths of "the hero with a thousand faces" each describes some odyssey to far places and strange lands—to Nyasaland, or the Kalahari, or outermost Siberia. Each tells the factual story of some individual journey, but each invests the factual story with the spirit of quest,

until the imagination suddenly invests the physical fact with
significance.

Consciously, van der Post has augmented his narrative of
journey in present time, with a second narrative of ancestral
journey through past time, until the three-dimensional geography
of space assumes another dimension. And as the "Journey In
Time" is added to the "Journey Through Space," the individual
journey becomes also a communal quest, to which the hero in-
vites the shades of his ancestors. Moreover, each individual
journey becomes a continuation and completion of each earlier
journey, until all become a part of the greater journey which is
history. But (and this is the unique aspect of van der Post's
writing) both the individual journey, and the communal journey
which is history, expand until they become part of a mythical
journey into "the lost world" of forgotten life which existed before conscious history and civilization began. To the three physical dimensions of geography, and the fourth temporal dimension
of history, he has added a fifth dimension of myth. And these
recurrent imaginative journeys into the unknown world of the
interior seem to retrace the immense journey of mankind backward toward his forgotten origins in prehistory.

Indeed, the essence of man's "immense journey" is exactly its
mythical timelessness. As Loren Eiseley,[1] who first used the
phrase, has suggested, the immense journey of man's physical
evolution toward civilized consciousness also implies the journey
of his conscious mind backward in time toward the understanding of his origins in prehistory. And the recurrent journeys, which
form the physical structure of van der Post's books, also imply
the journey of the imagination backward toward the understanding of origins.

This imaginative journey into the unconscious past naturally
involves mysticism. In his best books this remains implicit: the
reader is carried along by the physical story until, as if by magic,
he experiences a kind of illumination. Sometimes the mysticism
becomes explicit, and the reader—especially if he be literal
minded—may feel put upon. This is the danger of all mysticism.
But if these journeys into the interior are seen as part of man's
immense journey toward the understanding of his unconscious
origins, the mysticism and myth are seen as natural also. The
books not only describe the physical and conscious steps of all

these journeys, but also suggest their psychological and timeless aspects.

## I   Venture to the Interior

The title is significant: readers sometimes misquote "Journey
to the Interior." It is true that "Journey" would have described
both the physical substance and the psychological meaning of
the book. But where "Journey" would have implied a certain
plan and a safe end, "Venture" implies both uncertainty and
danger. The actual title suggests the pioneering adventure both
of the physical and of the psychological journeys, and of the
book itself. Both in substance and form, it is venturesome: there
is nothing quite like it in literature.

The unusual form is emphasized by the table of contents. The
book begins with a Preface, describing the author's state of mind
as he sits "in this restricted moment in time" in the London Air
Terminal awaiting the start of his journey of exploration to
Nyasaland. Part I, however, returns to describe "The Journey
in Time" accomplished by his ancestors, which has led to the
present "restricted moment" and which helps to explain his present disturbed state of mind. Part II then narrates the "Journey
through Space" which carries him by plane across Europe and
Northern Africa to Nyasaland, interspersing the narrative with
recollections of past experiences suggested by present circumstances. Parts III and IV narrate his actual explorations in Nyasaland, interspersed with other memories and associations. The
book ends matter-of-factly with the telegram: "All done and
hastening home."

This four-part structure is explicit and apparently simple. The
only unusual part is the first, "The Journey in Time," which is
quite brief but very effective. The other three parts seem mostly
straightforward narratives of the plane trip and of the two episodes of geographical exploration. After the vividly imagined
"Journey in Time" and the brilliantly narrated "Journey Through
Space," the reader may feel let down by the later narratives of
actual exploration. The return to earth—even the unexplored
earth of Africa—may seem routine. But the latter half of the
book gives substance to the earlier half, and also resolves the
conflicts introduced by it. Only when (in Chapter 21) the author
remembers, in the midst of the beauty of the African wilderness,

the cruelty of his prisoner-of-war experiences, is the interior violence finally converted into understanding.

More important than the explicit form of the book is its gradual and unobtrusive development of many different themes. On the level of physical realism, it tells of the actual journey and exploration in Africa. The narration is fast-paced and the description vivid. But on a second level, the book develops the character of the author by means of autobiography and personal reminiscence. Of deeper interest than the story of travel and adventure is the story of the development of personality: because the author's past experiences have made him a unique person, his present explorations become uniquely interesting. On a third level, however, past experiences interact with present circumstances, until the exploration of the interior wildness of Africa becomes also the exploration of the interior wildness of the heart of man. On this level the antique ritual of an orgiastic African dance (Chapter 23) acts out the violence hidden in the heart of civilized man, until the conscious recognition of it brings final resolution. The journey of exploration in time and through space becomes one with all journeys in all times, through ritual and myth. Finally, on the fourth level, this exploration of the interior wildness of both nature and man becomes also a journey in the discovery of meaning. Beyond the narrative of adventure, and the portraiture of autobiography, and the mythical exploration of the interior, the book suggests new psychological patterns and meanings. Later, these meanings will be developed explicitly in *The Dark Eye in Africa*. Here, they are wisely left implicit. But the mere adumbration of them gives *Venture* its final dimension and depth.

In addition to the formal division of *Venture* into four parts, the author has developed his meaning by means of a series of epigraphs, poetic quotations, mythical associations, and dreams. The epigraph to Part I is remarkably apt, invoking Sir Thomas Browne's: "We carry with us the wonders we seek without us: there is all Africa and her prodigies in us." Part I then describes the conflict of Africa and Europe in the lives of his parents, ending: "It presupposed, in its ultimate meaning, this among other journeys." The epigraph to Part II then generalizes the idea, quoting an old Swiss song: *"Notre vie est un voyage...."* For Part III the tragic implications of this ancestral conflict, and also of the present journey, are suggested by the epigraph from Gerald Manley Hopkins: "O the mind, mind has mountains, cliffs of fall. . . ." Then the simply descriptive title of Part III, "Encounter with the Mountain," acquires overtones of tragedy, both physical and psychological. Finally, the letter from Ingaret Giffard which prefaces Part IV emphasizes the "private and personal problems" which underlie the events of this journey, and of all others, whose working out the text now describes. Meanwhile, the final title, "Beyond the Mountain," suggests both the ultimate resolution of the conflict and the successful ending of the actual journey.

But the excellence of this book lies not so much in the clarity of its form or the originality of its technique, as in the skill with which the author has realized his purpose by means of narration and description. It is the duty of the critic to point out the skeleton of form, but the creative artist clothes the skeleton in living flesh. Although van der Post emphasizes his purpose by formal means, the reader easily forgets this in the development of the story. The physical venture into the heart of Africa continually holds his attention until, in the second half of the book, he may completely forget the psychological venture into the heart of man which is paralleling the physical story. But from the beginning in the Preface, the two stories are developed simultaneously and equally.

The five-page Preface is a masterpiece of brief exposition. Although most prefaces merely explain the purpose of the book, this one describes the beginning of the actual journey, narrates the events which led up to it, and even outlines the author's philosophy, before it emphasizes his fundamental purpose—to understand his own unconscious motives: "this other side of life coming up over the horizon of our consciousness, like a dark Homeric hull sailing before winds blowing from the uttermost limits of time." Then, even more briefly, it outlines the "unresolved conflict" within the author, between the unconscious "Africa" of his mother's heritage and the conscious "Europe" of his father's. But because this abstraction has already been particularized in the description of his present situation and his past experiences, it seems wholly real.

Part I returns to tell the story of his parents, partly in terms of history, partly of autobiography. The chapters describe each

parent as representative of South African history—the mother of
the pioneering drive of the Boers "deeper into the unknown interior of Southern Africa," and the father of the old, transplanted
European culture. But each parent is also related to the present
by means of autobiography—the mother to the son's love of ad-
venturous exploration, the father to his tragic sense of homeless-
ness, and questing: *"Nous cherchons notre passage/Dans le Ciel
ou rien ne luit."*

Part II then narrates "The Journey through Space" by airplane
from London to Nyasaland. This is the most vivid description of
a plane trip I know (even more vivid than Saint-Exupéry's),
and it somehow recalls Thomas Wolfe's description of his own
journey by train from Carolina to Boston. Both describe a "rite
of passage"—a transition both from one state of being to another,
and from one culture to another. But where Wolfe's description
was immediate and personal, van der Post's suggests long perspectives, both of space and of time. The changing landscapes
and changing time zones suggest the cultural changes, and the
autobiographical reminiscences suggest observations in depth.
But the most remarkable part of this "Journey through Space"
is that from Khartoum to Nairobi described in Chapter 5. The
actual plane flight from an outpost of Mediterranean civilization
into equatorial Africa is accompanied by a strange psychological
phenomenon: "The machine kept lurching, staggering and dropping unpredictably....The men starting drinking....For a while
something unexplained and irrational appeared to dominate the
actions of all of us....With my maps handy on my knees, I continued to look down with fierce concentration as if I expected
the haze and dust to vanish at any moment and a promised land
to appear." Shortly after landing at Nairobi, he remarks upon
the "queer, slight, but definitely somnambulistic air" of many
Europeans living in Kenya (a phenomenon also remarked by
Isak Dinesen earlier). The physical journey from Europe to
Africa has become a flight not only from European civilization
to African wildness, but from rational certainty to irrational fantasy: the "Journey through Space" has become also a "Journey
through Time" back to the primitive world which existed before
civilization began.

Part III seems wholly narrative and objective. Because the
author is exploring Nyasaland for the first time, there are few

reminiscences of past experiences. And because of his newness, he submits himself to the advice of the British officials who know this particular country. But progressively he suffers misgivings, which increase until suddenly the young British forester, Vance, is killed while attempting to ford a swollen mountain torrent. The native bearers are so overwhelmed by this disaster that they can be persuaded to continue only by dressing them in the extra clothes of the dead man. In "green, blue, red and gray striped pyjamas," they can laugh again, but the author is sick at heart at the incongruous spectacle. Afterwards he goes back in his mind to seek the causes of the tragedy. This black mountain has always been associated with legends of disaster, legends which long ago suggested Rider Haggard's fantasy of *The Children of the Mist.* There had been comments by British officials about the mountain: "terrific," "weird," "a wizard of a place." He remembers all his own ill-defined and half-conscious worries about the expedition. But most of all there had been his instinctive feeling about the character of young Vance himself—"so fantastically young and hurt"—a feeling later reinforced by the exclamation of the English lady with a houseful of cats: "I knew it would happen. I knew it. They just had something like it in them." He ends by blaming himself for not having heeded his own earlier premonitions and misgivings. Africa brings tragedy to those who act contrary to their own inner feelings.

Part IV continues this narrative of exploration. The author is prevented from flying by the same violent storm which had caused his earlier tragedy. Two British generals urge the pilot to disregard the weather, but the author—"a mere half-colonel"—overrides their urging. Instead he hires a car, and "for the first time I felt completely free of the cycle of events which started a week before." When the native chauffeur is terrified by the slippery road, he takes over. When he glimpses their objective, he perceives "a sort of Rider Haggard, a King Solomon's Mines, a Queen of Sheba touch about it." They are suddenly halted by a "young, black, female body, stark naked," lying on the road; but it proves to be not dead, but drunk, for it is harvest festival time. The expedition is later delayed by this spirit of festival; but eventually it succeeds, and its happy ending is celebrated by the primitive harvest dance of the bearers and their women beside the village fire in the night. Contrasted with the earlier bedraggled bearers dressed in striped pyjamas on the stormy mountain in the rain, these naked dancers have integrity. "Children of the darkness," they also possess "the wisdom of the dark."

The day after this dance the author and his friend meet a herd of wild zebra in the bright sunlight of the high Nyika plateau. The friend's duty is to shoot one zebra for scientific purposes, but he cannot bring himself to do it: "I just could not shoot, they were beautiful." The next night the author dreams of riding his black mare "at a thundering pace across the purple folds of the Nyika," and experiences a new "feeling of strength and security." Accepting the interior wildness of Africa, and accepting also the wildness within his own civilized nature, he finds new strength and peace.

From civilization Thoreau had proclaimed: "In wildness is the preservation of the world." Van der Post has explored the ultimate wildness of the interior of Africa and has experienced its power of preservation. But best of all, he has narrated these experiences in a book free of all moralism and abstraction.

## II  The Dark Eye in Africa

To read *The Dark Eye in Africa* after *Venture to the Interior* is to be impressed with the importance of literary form. *Venture* has become a modern classic because (among other things) its form realizes a literary idea of great originality and power. But where *Venture* was carefully constructed, *The Dark Eye*, apparently, "just growed." In its latest American edition (1960) it consists of two Introductions, one "Basis for Discussion," a long "Discussion" comprising twenty-one brief "Questions" and extended "Answers," and a concluding "Author's Note." Except for the original lecture, or "Basis for Discussion," the book is essentially formless. It even renounces journalistic accuracy by admitting that some of the "Questions" were asked at later offerings of the original lecture.

But if *The Dark Eye* lacks the virtue of form, it possesses other major virtues. It is full of original ideas and illuminating insights. And, even more important, it is charged with the speaking presence of the author. Each idea is related to its origins in experience and is realized through his feeling of personal involvement. The autobiographical realism which *Venture* conveyed in the form of narrative is here conveyed by the image of the author speaking. The long succession of Questions and Answers vividly suggests the author's active relationship with his present audience. And because he is, in actual life, at his best in personal relationships, and speaks with great eloquence, the impression of personal immediacy is wholly real. The seeming formlessness is partly intentional.

Moreover, *The Dark Eye* possesses the great virtue of style, and, proverbially, "the style is the man." One quotation may illustrate the combination of colloquial immediacy, autobiographical realism and mytho-poetic suggestion with which this book abounds:

This picture which I have given you is vanishing fast, though it is still valid in large tracts of the great continent. The bushman is still living in the Kalahari Desert, just as he did in the beginning of time. I have recently been there and I have seen him in his natural and innocent society, still using his love-making ritual, the cupid's bow, which hitherto for me had been little more than an image on a Greek vase. I have also been in sleeping-sickness country just below the great escarpments of Abyssinia and seen black people of superb physique, garlands of wild flowers round their necks, marching towards me unexpectedly out of the singing grass and playing on pipes exactly like the Pipes of Pan which, too, I had only known from Greek vases.

The author is consciously presenting his audience with "this picture" of Africa, then illustrating it from his own past personal experiences and, finally, illuminating it with vignettes from antique art and mythology.

In spite of formal differences, *The Dark Eye* describes essentially the same idea which *Venture* had narrated. Both develop the epigraph from Sir Thomas Browne: "We carry with us the wonders we seek without us: there is all Africa and her prodigies in us." In more prosaic words, "Africa" is both a state of mind and a condition of man, as well as a geographical continent; the symbolic location of the heart of darkness and of the aboriginal nature of man. Put in terms of Jungian psychology, Africa is the home of the "collective unconscious" which European man has banished from his civilization and has repressed from his individual consciousness. Nevertheless, European man still carries this unconscious "Africa" about within him.

The author begins by limiting this "Africa" to the part of the continent which lies south of the Sahara (North Africa has become part of European civilization). The recent opening of this uncivilized Africa to commerce with European civilization has caused great unrest; but this "African" unrest is more than political, and, indeed, more than African. It not only includes the discontent of Africans with European rulers, but also the discontent of all men with civilization itself. It includes the unrest of non-Western peoples with Western colonialism, and of liberal-minded people with the established order. "African" unrest is, therefore, a world-wide state of mind. But it is a state of mind conditioned by the fact that the African continent continues to nourish an aboriginal "African" state of nature.

The section of *The Dark Eye* which describes this aboriginal Africa, and speculates on the reasons for its continued survival in our modern civilized world, contains some of van der Post's best writing. "Africa is old in the longest measure of time on earth. . . ." He cites the speculations of geologists that Africa was once part of a great southern land mass named "Gondwanaland, a name which has an odd gone-with-the-wind nostalgia implicit in its sound," which broke off long aeons ago from the northern land mass and still retains wholly different species of rocks and plants and animals. He describes how the deserts and mountains of Africa have formed defenses which "completely sealed Africa off from the outer world," and how "nature developed the most redoubtable champions in the mosquito and tsetse fly and other minute parasites, all able to strike down any invader." Thus Africa became the fortress of original life which still preserves thousands of unique species of animal and man, together with antique ways of life long since destroyed by civilization in Europe and Asia.

"But suddenly we, European man, burst in upon this scene." After a century or two of skirmishes which easily established the supremacy of Europeans, the Africans soon ceased to resist. "In the African heart there was a calm and tense air of expectation of growing wonders to come, and as a result there was also the most moving and wonderful readiness of the African to serve, to imitate and to follow the European." But during the last century this readiness to follow has been dissipated by the failure of the European to lead. Frustration and despair have created blind resentment and an inner violence. The light of hope in African eyes has darkened, and the inner violence has resulted in occasional sudden explosions of individual violence, and of tribal violence such as the Mau-Mau. The dark eye has become general in Africa.

Thus far the author has generalized from history and from actual experience; now he begins to develop new ideas, related to those of Jungian psychology. The darkening of the eye in modern Africa has not been limited to the black man, or, indeed, to Africa. The same frustration and inner despair has led in Europe to the violence of world wars, and to sudden blind explosions of individual crime. The eye of modern man has darkened throughout the world.

In Europe the darkness of man's inner nature has always been recognized, but its expression has been suppressed by European civilization. In aboriginal Africa, however, it has not been suppressed, but has been allowed expression in tribal warfare, ritual, dance, and myth. Civilized man, therefore, has come to associate the dark and savage aspect of his inner nature with Africa. And because Africans have had black skins, Europeans have associated the black skin with the black heart. They have confused the outer blackness of Africans with the inner blackness of man's nature. Racial prejudice has been the result.

"Now the white man in Africa sees reflected in the natural dark man round him that dark aspect of himself which he has rejected." In a later essay van der Post has entitled this phenomenon: "Race Prejudice as Self-Rejection." Here he concludes this essay by suggesting that "the unrest in Africa, in all its facets . . . is plainly an extension of our own individual unrest." And he illustrates from autobiographical experience: "I discovered that I traveled Africa in this way because it brought me to unknown places in my own uncomprehended spirit which I could not have reached in any other manner. Perhaps therein reside the miracle and meaning of Africa for all of us."

In his next book, *The Lost World of the Kalahari,* van der Post continued his explorations of the primitive Africa of man's "uncomprehended spirit." But through the long "Discussion" which concludes *The Dark Eye,* he returns to answer the objections of practical-minded people to his ideas, and to illustrate by incidents from his own life, from history and from mythology. In the American edition this "Discussion" is arranged to begin and end with the more practical questions. But many "Answers" are devoted to the illustration of his ideas from mythology; and these illustrations, which constitute the climax of the English edition, are grouped in the middle of the American edition.

In the American edition, the first eight Questions and Answers clarify the author's ideas. His interpretation of "African unrest" as part of the unrest of all modern civilization has the practical virtue, he suggests, of relieving "us, *in part,* of an impossible burden of responsibility." He explains that "I left economics out of this talk," not because economics are unimportant, but because the causes of the violence of "the dark eye" are psychological. And he answers an objection to his own earlier assertion that the black man has really valued white civilization and has really wished to be led, by quoting the words of his Sudanese camel-driver in Abyssinia: "I can remember how it was here before the government came." This incident from autobiographical experience (also remembered in *Venture to the Interior*) illuminates both African history and psychology.

The next seven Questions and Answers (Questions 9 to 15 in the American edition) go beyond the original text to develop, rather than merely to clarify, the author's ideas. They develop his suggestions that a nation's mythology may prefigure its history. This mythological interpretation of life and history is largely inspired by Jungian psychology, but is here enlarged and applied to the problems of Africa and the modern world in a series of original and illuminating insights. These "Answers" outline some ideas which his later books and lectures will develop more fully (and which will be discussed in the last chapter of this book). The first four, concluding with the legend of a white queen dwelling somewhere in the unknown interior of Africa, form the climax of the English edition. But the next three, which develop the author's personal myth of his own continuing journey into the interior, develop these legends further and suggest the possible transcendence of national and racial history by enlightened individuals.

The long "Answer" which compares the German myth of a superior race to the South African myth of "a God-chosen people" is rich in suggestion. Not only does it explain the South African sympathy for Nazi Germany, but it also suggests comparisons with the American myth of manifest destiny. "The first book written in Afrikaans argued that the original garden of Eden was in the heart of Africa," and "the Great Trek through a great unknown wilderness to a land of promise" sought to rediscover this Eden in Africa, much as Americans sought to rediscover it in America. Therefore, although the German myth ended in a disastrous *"Goetterdaemmerung,"* the Afrikaaner myth (like the American) envisions a transcendence of past evil and disaster. This "New Testament myth" of a paradise to be regained leads to the climactic myth of the white queen who rules over the instincts of her dark subjects somewhere in the unknown interior.

With this myth of the white queen, van der Post ended his book in its English edition. But his American editors rearranged the "Discussion" so that in the American edition his confession of faith followed the legend of the white queen: "I still have faith in the power of the myth which brought my countrymen to Africa and compelled them to set out on their great journey to the interior." And the later "Discussion" in the American edition continues: "The spirit of man is nomad, his blood Bedouin, his being is frontiersman . . ." This discussion of the mythological meaning of history then concludes "that we are all chosen people charged in our unique and several ways to bring the journey to its contracted end, our differences honourable, equal in dignity. . . ." The American edition concludes with a series of minor "Answers" to specific "Questions" or objections. The author is not anti-intellectual: "I believe most profoundly in the increase of consciousness." He is a realist: under present conditions, interracial marriages are not likely to succeed. He answers an English woman: "You must not allow yourselves to hate us in Africa." Finally, there is a long discussion of "the American angle."

But whatever the order of "Discussion" and whatever the edition, *The Dark Eye* remains a kind of "Work in Progress." It possesses all the virtues and all the faults of a living discussion of new ideas which are being imagined and formulated for the first time. Illustrated by personal experience and related to national history, it goes back to literature and mythology to suggest new answers to the problems of Africa, and of all the contemporary world.

### III  The Lost World of the Kalahari

Like *Venture to the Interior*, *The Lost World of the Kalahari*
(1958) describes an actual journey of exploration by the author
to a remote region of Africa. Like *Venture*, it also describes a
"journey in time" back into childhood and beyond, to the historic time when the author's ancestors first landed at the Cape
of Good Hope to encounter the Bushmen who had first inhabited the country. Like *Venture* also, it describes a journey in
consciousness toward the understanding of these aboriginal
Africans who lived before civilization began.

But this journey of exploration to the Kalahari is subtly different from that described in *Venture*. Most significantly, it has
been planned and organized by the author, rather than assigned
to him by the government. This will explore "the lost world"
of the Bushmen who had flourished in prehistoric Africa, before
the savage Bantu tribes of modern times had migrated down
from the northern interior. Consequently this "journey in time"
is longer, beginning with childhood memory but continuing far
back into the mythical time before history began. And this journey in consciousness is even more venturesome, exploring the
heart—not so much of the author and of the tribesmen of modern Africa—as of the aboriginal African hunters of prehistory.

*The Lost World of the Kalahari* is simpler and more direct
in form than *Venture to the Interior*. There is no division into
Parts, to separate the "journey in time" from the "journey
through space." Where *Venture* emphasized the multiple meanings of "the interior," one can read *The Lost World* without
explicit awareness that its action is more than physical. The
autobiographical references remain more personal and the history more factual. Although the author mentions earlier expeditions, the book focuses entirely on this one, and the narrative
achieves sharper focus. Where *Venture* had described journeys
to different places, *The Lost World* has unity of place. Some
readers prefer it because of this unity and apparent simplicity;
it tells a vivid, straightforward story of an expedition of
exploration.

Yet fast-paced in narration and vivid in description, *The Lost
World* nevertheless omits many of the sensory details which
popular books of exploration usually emphasize. To compare
*The Lost World of the Kalahari* with *Kalahari Sand* by Frank

Debenham (the book which describes the earlier, official explorations of this desert) is to realize that, where the earlier explorer had emphasized the physical details of his expeditions, van der Post takes the desert almost for granted. Debenham described the millions of bugs which infested the encampment by night, the suffocating clouds of dust which enveloped their moving trucks, and the fever that attacked him with debilitating effect. But van der Post emphasizes the psychological effects. I do not recall any description of his own physical discomfort during the expedition, although later, when I asked him if he had met Elisabeth Marshall Thomas (author of *The Harmless People*), he replied: "No, but I met her father in the Kalahari and envied him his beautiful, air-conditioned truck." Toward the end of *The Lost World* he describes a Bushman hunter who easily hurdled over an angry cobra while racing in pursuit of an eland; and like him, the author takes all such routine dangers in stride.

This book focuses, not upon the exploration of the Kalahari desert, but rather upon the unique Bushman hunters who once ranged over all South Africa but who have now retreated into the innermost center of this last desert. The first chapter recalls the author's childhood memories of the Bushmen. The tenth and last chapter narrates his farewell to the tiny group of "pure" Bushmen whom he had finally discovered in the heart of the desert. The chapters between describe his gradual discovery of "the lost world" of these Bushmen, whose diminished remnants survive only here.

The first two chapters seem to me the best. They recall "the lost world" of the title, suggesting the symbolic identity of the author's lost childhood with the way of life of the Bushmen who lived in the childhood of the human race. "Perhaps this life of ours which begins as the quest of the child for the man, and ends as a journey of the man to rediscover the child, needs a clear image of some child-man, like the Bushman, wherein the two are firmly and lovingly joined." Combining childhood reminiscence with observed fact, this chapter paints a bright picture of a unique people. Like "the journey in time," which introduces *Venture to the Interior*, this is rich in autobiography and African lore.

Chapter Two, "The Manner of Their Going," achieves the even more difficult task of making past history come vividly alive. Its

description of "the terror, destruction and disintegration, like
the smell of the dead rotting on an apocalyptic battle field,"
which followed the simultaneous attack on the Bushmen by the
Blacks from the North and the Whites from the South, rises to
an eloquence rare in historical writing. And the feeling of terror
is driven home by the tales told by family servants of a canni-
balism "so close to my own day that as a child I was possessed
by the fear of being eaten by cannibals." The manner of the destruction of the Bushmen was even more violent than that of the
American Indians. But the Bushmen had created a way of life
more unique, and a culture far higher than that of the Indians.

The third chapter is purely autobiographical. It describes the
author's continuing fascination with the Bushmen, and his dream
in a Japanese prison, which in a sense prophesied this expedition and imbued it with the spirit of quest. The fourth chapter
then describes the planning and the personnel of the new expedition. Comparison with Debenham's earlier *Kalahari Sand* again
emphasizes the psychological depth of van der Post's book.
Debenham had described the personnel of the earlier expedition
(including "Van") in terms of present performance and personality; but van der Post describes his own personnel (one of whom
had also been with Debenham) in terms of life-experience—
especially experience of wild Africa. Only Spode, the first camera-man, who is to cause all the trouble, had lacked experience
of Africa and its savagery.

The next three chapters narrate the difficulties and near-
tragedy caused by the alienation of Spode, the European. These
difficulties correspond to the tragedy described in Part Three of
*Venture to the Interior,* entitled "Encounter with the Mountain."
The cause is much the same: both Vance, the English forester
in *Venture,* and Spode, the European camera-man in *The Lost
World,* had suffered in European life, and had come to Africa
as a land of opportunity, without in any way understanding its
dangers. Both are "accident-prone" as it were: each "had tragedy
in him." Vance had been swept over the waterfall, and Spode
now wallows in a psychological slough of despond. But in this
new book the psychological pattern is left implicit, while the
narrative advances swiftly and objectively.

The character of Spode forms the perfect foil to that of the
author. The oversensitive European has suffered in the war, like

the author, and is also attracted to Africa. But he cannot cope
with its wildness. He retreats into egotism and self-pity, blaming
his failure on others: "But Laurens, you do not ever understand."
He has brought along his violin "to play for the lions at night,"
but after one performance beside the fire, he abandons it. *"Mais,
c'est trop sauvage."* Gradually he retreats wholly into himself
and refuses all activity, while the expedition simultaneously bogs
down physically in "The Swamp of Despond." Only after Spode
is shipped home to Europe can the expedition begin to succeed.

But the shadow of European tragedy continues to haunt them.
The chapter entitled "The Spirits of Slippery Hills" narrates a
series of incidents so extraordinary that it almost strains the
limits of belief, and it ends with a ritual so irrational that some
of the white participants even are moved to protest. The moral—
which is never made explicit—is that the European must submit
himself to the ways of the wild before he can hope to discover
its "lost world." But the action is narrated objectively, and the
reader is left to draw his own conclusions. Consider the following incidents.

First the author persuades a South African camera-man to join
the expedition in place of the European Spode, and with a
"tame" Bushman for guide they all start for the inner desert.
But the author had promised the Bushman not to allow any
killing of game on the way to the ancient Bushman sanctuary.
Then in his troubles with Spode he had forgotten his promise,
and now his friends shoot a steenbock. This violent breaking of
a sacred taboo disturbs the guide, and when they reach the
ancient Bushman paintings at "Slippery Hills," the guide tries
to pray but falls backward as if rebuffed by the spirits. The next
morning they are attacked by an angry swarm of bees, like a
plague out of Egypt. When the new camera-man tries to film
the rock paintings, his camera jams, and soon after the whole
camera breaks. Then the Bushman guide consults "the spirits"
in a strange ceremony: "They are angry because you have come
here with blood on your hands." At last van der Post writes a
letter "To The Spirits": "We beg most humbly the pardon of the
great spirits of these Slippery Hills." And he persuades his
friends to sign also. Only when the rational-minded white men
thus humble themselves before "the spirits" of "the lost world"
can they rediscover that world.

The last two chapters now tell the story of the actual discovery of "the lost world of the Kalahari." They narrate the trip to the central desert and the meeting with a group of "pure" Bushmen living there. They describe the steps by which the author gradually gains the confidence of these "pure" Bushmen: only by submitting himself to their ways and attitudes can he accomplish this. First the Bushmen show him the physical processes by which they suck water out of the deep sand at "The Sip Wells," and the external routines of their living. Then the final chapter describes the climactic events leading to the telling of their sacred myths, and their dancing of thanksgiving after the hunt and after the rain.

The ending of this book, like its beginning, is more psychological than historical. The first eight chapters have described the difficulties to be overcome before "the lost world" can be discovered. Although these difficulties have been real, the true subject has not been the physical journey through space, but the psychological journey in consciousness, back to an understanding of the world of the prehistoric Bushmen. The crucial chapter has described the victory of "The Spirits of the Slippery Hills" over the modern mentality of the white men. The ninth chapter begins: "I have no intention of attempting to explain these events now except to mention . . . their consequences within myself." Having accepted the taboos and beliefs of "the lost world," he is able to discover it. And having discovered it, it seems as if he had also rediscovered the lost world of his own childhood: "The child in me had become reconciled to the man."

## IV  The Heart of the Hunter

"*The Heart of the Hunter* begins where *The Lost World of the Kalahari* left off. We are on our way out of the Central Desert." In the Introduction to this new book, published in 1961, the author explains his problem in writing his "continuation": the narrative describes the ending of the earlier journey, but "when this journey out of the desert ended . . . I discovered that in a sense the journey had hardly begun." The new book therefore describes two separate journeys—the physical one, along with the new and more difficult journey in search of the meaning of the lost world whose physical remnants had just been discovered. "I find the thought of what Black and White did to the Bushman almost more than I can endure . . . Yet it seemed to me some atonement would be accomplished if I helped to see that the meaning his life held for him would not perish as he perished." *The Heart of the Hunter* focuses upon the "heart" of the Bushman, and the final section explores the inner meaning of his lost world, as expressed in Bushman mythology.

In terms of conventional form, therefore, this is really two separate books. The first describes the physical journey out of the Central Desert, the second evokes the meaning which life held for the aboriginal African hunter long before the eye of Africa began to darken. Where *Venture to the Interior* had been narrative, and *The Dark Eye* had been interpretive, *The Heart of the Hunter* is half one and half the other. The Introduction declares independence of conventional form: "I hope I have learned by now the danger and futility of trying to improve on one's own truth. So the shape of this book is not imposed on the story from without, but is determined solely by the way the experience came to me." The new, unconventional form is basically autobiographical, but it has already been suggested by the earlier books of non-fiction, where the physical act has revealed the meaning by means of symbolic form. But now the meaning can no longer be suggested by means of conventional symbol, because the journey to this lost world has spanned an abyss between the modern world and the prehistoric world of the hunter. To the aboriginal hunter life meant something radically different than to modern civilized man. "I had a feeling that I was possibly the only person who could start this kind of interpretation."

Thus *The Heart of the Hunter* attempts to solve a literary problem of great difficulty. The book is not always easy to read, and the final Part is often difficult to understand. But its challenge is exciting, and its insight illuminating. Although the Bushman myths often seem strange to the point of incomprehensibility, the author's interpretations of them often illuminate the meaning of life in this lost world. Consider, for example, the mythical battle between the Bushman god and the baboons. In one of the myths of early creation, the Bushman god sends his son to do battle with the baboons, who are always bickering with him. But the baboons batter his son so hard that his eyeball falls out, and the son dies, whereupon they seize the eyeball and play catch with it. The god then comes, and although he cannot over-come the baboons, he rescues his son's eyeball, which he then immerses in the water beside a spring, until the son is resurrected from this death. Van der Post then explains that for the Bushman, these bickering baboons symbolized the critical intellect, which separates the organ of vision from its living context, and care-lessly plays games with it, destroying its vital function. The troublesome baboons cannot be beaten at their own game, and the divine vision can only be recovered and renewed in a new context.

The author's interpretation of this myth seems persuasive, and indeed almost self-evident. Yet the casting of the baboon in the role of the critical intellect seems strange to the modern mind. For instance, if someone should call me a "big baboon," I would not take it as a compliment to my critical intelligence. On the contrary: in our modern, man-centered world, the baboon has become the symbol of brute stupidity. But in the Bushman's animal-centered world, the baboon seemed the most intellectual of all the animals. Between this natural world of the hunter and the self-conscious world of the modern scientist an abyss exists, and the bickering baboon, the confused man-animal living mid-way between the two worlds, gets it from both sides. In the lost world of the Bushman, where man was a hunting animal among other animals, nature was the measure of all things. In the mod-ern world man lives apart from the animals, and man separated from nature has become the measure of all things.

The author's growing realization of the abyss which separates these two worlds gives an autobiographical unity to *The Heart of the Hunter*, to compensate for its diversity of literary form. Part I describes the world of the Bushman hunter in physical terms, but emphasizes its strangeness. Part II narrates the au-thor's experiences of the "World Between," emphasizing the radical separateness of the two worlds. Part III, "World Re-gained," describes the author's growing understanding of the meaning of the lost world, by means of an interpretation of its myths.

The beautiful dust jacket of the original edition of the book pictures the black profile of a young Bushman mother holding her infant son in her arms, standing on a brown desert and gaz-ing up at a blue desert sky bright with stars. Sketched originally by the author himself, this picture represents an incident narrated at the beginning of the story, and catches perfectly the mood of the book as a whole. The Bushman is giving expression to man's aboriginal feeling of reverence before the god of nature. Dabé, the tame Bushman, explains: "She is asking the stars to take from her little child his little heart and to give him the heart of the hunter." Both the narrative incident and the dust jacket which represents it realize the simple spirit of unity between aboriginal man and wild nature, and suggest the strangeness of that spirit to the divided mind of modern man.

The succeeding chapters describe a variety of incidents occurring during the journey out of the Central Desert towards civilization. Vivid and strange in themselves, they are given focus by reference to the troubled mind of Dabé, the tame Bushman. Torn between identification with the wild Bushmen whom he is leaving, and association with the civilized world which he is now approaching, his actions reveal his inner torment and he progressively confides to the sympathetic author his fears of the life to which he is returning. Although he had earlier guided the expedition to its discovery of the "pure" Bushmen at the Sip Wells, his character had not been developed in the earlier book. Now the division within his heart foreshadows the author's own realization of this division in the "World Between," which follows upon his own return to civilization. Meanwhile Dabé becomes the vehicle for the interpretation of the Bushman hunter.

These chapters include a wealth of incident drawn from earlier expeditions and of story narrated by other members of this expedition. "Man and Desert" sketches the characters of Europeans who have "gone native" among the Bushmen: of Tom Hardbattle, who loved the desert purely, and of the Australian renegade who found in it escape from the puritanical inhibitions of his childhood. "The desert can be all things to man, but above all it is a symbol of what has been most deeply denied in men's own spirit." These "European Bushmen" share with Dabé, the "tame Bushman," the division of spirit caused by civilized man's rejection of the natural world.

Part II, "World Between," describes several incidents of this rejection. After returning to civilization, Dabé and another Black are subjected to a tongue-lashing by the local station-master, because they sit upon benches traditionally reserved for whites

—despite the fact that this is in Bechuanaland, outside the juris-
diction of South Africa. *Apartheid* has spread even to the desert
to deny the Bushman his natural human dignity, and he is bewildered by a hostility he cannot understand. Similarly, the author finds at this frontier outpost a Bushman woman who has
suffered degradation after her husband has been taken to prison
for an offense against a law he could not understand. As Dabé
explains it: "The time of the Hyena is upon her." Having been
denied his humanity by civilized law, the Bushman heart is
dying, and the symbolic scavengers of nature are waiting.

Now the author carries out his earlier promise to Dabé to
"speak to the government." In answer to the Commissioner's
objection that the Bushman is "of no use" to civilization, he
points out that the wild animal life of Africa is equally "useless,"
but it has been given sanctuary in Parks and Reservations.
Should not the Bushman be treated as well as the wild animals?
Yet a Reservation is only another form of *apartheid*, and the very
nature of the hunter's life unfits him for life in civilization. Only
by understanding "the heart of the hunter" can modern man find
any "use" for him.

Chapter Ten returns to childhood reminiscence and autobiography to suggest the ultimate meaning of the Bushman—not as
physical fact but as archetypal symbol. The author's lectures
describing him have always stirred the imaginations of audiences
in all countries: they "wrote to me saying they had dreamt about
the Bushman after first hearing me talk about him." He seemed
to "represent some elemental common denominator in such diversity of spirit . . . the child before whom we are commanded to
humble ourselves and to become like if we are to enter the
Kingdom."

Part III, "World Regained," remembers the tales told by his
Bushman nurse in childhood and records the myths collected
during his recent expedition. Adding to older Bushman material
collected by earlier scholars, the author uses these myths to
interpret the heart of the hunter. Their strangeness sometimes
makes them difficult to understand, but it contributes to their
fascination. The stories are arranged to suggest a "natural progression toward greater awareness in the mind of the first people
of Africa," but this progression sometimes evades the reader.
The interpretation of the individual myths, however, often sug-

gests brilliant insights. The battle of the baboons, described above, is one example. But the central figure of Bushman mythology was the praying mantis.

The first god of the Bushman was not a human being, of course, for the hunter's world was not anthropomorphic. But the god was not even a powerful animal—not lion, or tiger, or elephant. At the very opposite extreme, the Bushman god was an insect, who by his natural stance suggested an attitude of prayer. The least of all the creatures of nature, he embodied the virtues of reverence and humility. Unable to conquer the animal kingdom, he lived by submitting to nature and following her ways.

The series of myths which constitute "The Saga of Mantis" suggest a bewildering kaleidoscope of shapes and colors, which the author-interpreter translates into strange new meanings. Besides Mantis, the cast of characters includes Porcupine, "the Rainbow," Dassie the rock-rabbit, the Blue Crane, "the All-Devourer," and a host of other animals and phenomena of nature. To the collection and interpretation of these aboriginal fantasies the author had devoted many years, and two books. A friend once expressed his own mixture of perplexity and admiration: "Imagine a man spending ten years of his life trying to interpret the meaning of a grasshopper!"

The praying mantis is not technically a grasshopper, yet the comparison is natural. The mere fact that an insignificant insect much like a grasshopper was the first god of the Bushman almost needed ten years of interpretation. The mythical conflict of this god Mantis with his great adversary, the All-Devourer, needs less interpretation, because unlike Mantis, the All-Devourer is as familiar to us as he was to the Bushmen in the Stone Age. But an idea suggests itself: might this All-Devourer have represented to the Bushmen the dark and destructive aspect of Mantis, the grasshopper-like god? Right or wrong, the idea may suggest the fascination of the new avenues of thought opened by this book.

## V  A View of All the Russias

*A View of All the Russias* (1964) is the only book by van der Post seemingly not inspired by his own inner experience. He had served a long apprenticeship as journalist on several South African newspapers, but none of his earlier books had been journalistic. Now his trip to Russia had been commissioned by

*Holiday* magazine, and his descriptions of it had been serialized in that magazine. The organization and the style of the book reflect this background; it is addressed to the widest possible audience and it contains the fewest undertones of inner meaning, suggesting no "venture to the interior" but only a clear overview of an alien country. For this reason the American title seems more appropriate than the English: it is "A View of" rather than a "Journey into" Russia.

But if the book is journalistic, it is inspired journalism. Like all his other books, it reflects the author's personality and his intense concern with human relationships and values. As different as possible from the conventional journalism which describes external facts and statistics, this describes personal meetings and conversations with a rich variety of Russian people in different situations. It gives at first hand the "feel" of Russia, and reflects the author's intense desire to understand and to like the country.

Paradoxically, the book derives its greatest power from its descriptions of why the author failed to like Soviet Russia. Throughout a lifetime of varied experiences in many countries of different cultures—from modern Japan to the aboriginal Bushmen—he had never before failed to feel at home in a foreign land. Even though he had always been repelled by doctrinaire communism, he had believed that men of all countries and races could achieve understanding through sincere personal relationships. Both in practice and in theory he had succeeded in realizing this ideal, refusing to hate the Japanese during the war and renewing his friendships with them afterwards. Now he visited Russia with the intention of talking with individual Russians on a level deeper than that of politics and economics. His book describes these meetings, and the partial failure of these talks.

The talks failed, partly because many Soviet citizens identified themselves exclusively with economics and politics. When visiting the immense new hydroelectric dam near Bratsk he conversed with several workers, but found that they would admit to no desires or values beyond those connected with the success of their project. "They had picked up the hydro-electric disease and experienced a sense of superiority and satisfaction in practicing this snobbery." That is to say, the materialism which Marxism had always preached had now become accepted as the only standard of value by many Russians.

Negatively, however, his most promising talks with Russians—especially Russian artists and writers—failed for a different reason. Artists often accepted the anti-materialistic values which differentiate art from propaganda everywhere, and as private citizens they were sometimes willing to discuss these values. But always at some point in the conversations the Russian artists found it necessary to retire behind the protective barrier of silence which the state imposed upon the free discussion of ideas—especially with foreigners. The most interesting and moving passages in this book describe the partial successes of the author's many attempts to get below the surface of the Russian mind and to discover its deepest beliefs and values.

The organizing principle of the book, however, is geographical and physical, rather than artistic and intellectual. It first describes the author's flight from London to Moscow, then his four subsequent trips from Moscow to different parts of the Soviet Union—to four different "Russias." Each trip, and each different city or region, is described in a series of chapters which include a mixture of personal impressions, vignettes of past history, talks with officials and with private individuals along the way, and interpretations of these experiences and conversations by the author. The result is a rich variety of travel writing, unified by the author's personality and ideas.

The book begins much as *Venture to the Interior* began—with "the mood which I took on the journey to Russia. For years I had been in trouble with the image of Russia presented to us in the outside world." Now, having completed his own Venture to the Interior, he seeks to compare this exterior image of Russia with the observed reality.

From the time of first boarding the Russian plane in London, to the time of boarding the British plane in Moscow for the return flight home, the narrative emphasizes the differences between Russian and Western life. The Russian stewardesses do not smile a professional welcome, but later show genuine friendliness on informal occasions. The Russian cab driver expresses immense pride in the ugly square apartments newly built by the state on the outskirts of Moscow. But above all the book describes the endless, inflexible regulations imposed by the state and obeyed without question by all, except a few artists and outsiders.

The most interesting incidents are those which occur outside
European Russia. In Tashkent a colony of Communist students
from Asian countries welcome the chance to talk with an out-
sider, and to confess their lonely disillusion—not with communism, but with "the unqualified assumption in the official life
around that Soviet values were absolutes." "My Young Friends in
Yalta" also confess their longing for news of the art and literature of the outside world, and ridicule the Soviet commissars of
art—one of whose spies they suspect of eavesdropping on this
conversation. On "Train Number Two" into Siberia, a Chinese
delegation becomes progressively cheerful as it approaches the
Chinese border. And in the Far East a young Russian guide
quotes Kipling to emphasize his feeling of the abyss between
China and Russia.

But the climax of the book comes at the end, in Moscow.
Another group of "young friends" has spent the last evening with
the author discussing literature, praising Pasternak, and reciting
new poems by the young Voznesensky and others. The atmosphere has seemed gay and hopeful. Nevertheless, on departure
the next day regulations have clamped down again, and the
author is forced to depart alone and incommunicado.

On the wall of the living room of the author's home in London
there hangs a "self-portrait" in oil by a nameless Soviet painter.
The natural outlines of the face are obscured by a cross-hatching
of right-angled lines, dots, and smudges. The individual human
face seems to be struggling to emerge from a confused, inhuman
background, which almost obliterates its identity. The denial of
freedom which causes this loss of identity is the basic theme of
A View of All the Russias. But the ideal achievement of perfect
human identity through experience of all human conditions and
cultures has been the theme of all van der Post's books.

## CHAPTER 5

# Fiction: "To the Heart of Darkness"

V AN DER POST'S first novel begins: "At the age of twenty-
five Johan van Bredepoel fell seriously ill for the first time in
his life." The illness proves to be psychosomatic, and the rest of
the novel explores the causes of it. Similarly his second novel
begins: "When 'the crisis,' as he called it afterwards, occurred
in the life of David Alexander Michaeljohn . . ." The fourth novel
describes a similar spiritual illness under the title: "The Growth
of Nothing." But whatever the name of the trouble, and whatever its symptoms, some dark melancholia lies at the heart of
these novels. *The Dark Eye in Africa* had sought to analyze this
same inner darkness, but most of his books of non-fiction had
described some journey *into* the interior, rather than the inner
darkness itself. The novels concentrate on the heart of darkness.

Perhaps this difference in emphasis explains why his books of
non-fiction have often proved more successful than his novels.
It is easier to narrate a venture into the interior than to describe
the interior itself. The physical journey involves a swift-moving
narrative with an accompanying sense of progress; but the interior must be described (rather than narrated), and its darkness
depicted. To focus upon darkness requires the genius of a Rem-
brandt or a Conrad. And at their best, van der Post's novels
depict this kind of luminous darkness.

But they approach this darkness by different paths, and they
describe it in different shapes. In technique the novels range
from the realistic to the symbolic, and in subject matter from the
tale of extravagant adventure to that of psychological compulsion. *In A Province* conforms to the traditional pattern of the
well-made realistic novel. *The Face Beside the Fire* combines
symbolism with psychological suggestion. *Flamingo Feather* tells
a flamboyant adventure story, with overtones of mystery. *The*

*Seed and the Sower* combines three separate novellas set in war-time Indonesia, but connects them by a common theme. *The Hunter and the Whale* tells a story of epic scope and psychological depth. The variety of these novels, therefore, seems more important than their similarity: the darkness lies only at the heart.

## I   In A Province

*In A Province* occupies a unique position among the author's books: it is the only one written before the war and belongs clearly to the historical era of the Great Depression. Moreover, it is the author's only book in the purely realistic tradition; the others all partake of symbolism in technique or of mysticism in philosophy. This one grew directly out of his early experience of racial injustice and political repression in South Africa, and is part of the world-wide literature of social protest. It was directly inspired by his friend William Plomer's novel, *Turbott Wolfe*. When it first appeared in 1934 it was highly praised, and has been reprinted in several new editions since. Everyone agrees that it is a very good novel, and some critics consider it his best.

The specific quality of this novel is emphasized by Ezekiel Mphahlele in his book, *The African Image*. Among those novels which have contributed to "The White Man's Image of the Non-White in Fiction," Mphahlele gives high place to *In A Province*, second only to *Turbott Wolfe*, and above Alan Paton's *Cry, the Beloved Country*. He then adds: "I still consider *In A Province* the best fiction he [van der Post] ever wrote. He has become a mystic. Apart from a portion of his volume of lectures, *The Dark Eye in Africa*, he is quite unintelligible to me."[1] Since Mr. Mphahlele is a sophisticated critic (who condemns *Cry, the Beloved Country* for its "flat, easily labeled characters," like those of *Uncle Tom's Cabin*), and since his opinion is shared by others, it is worth examining in detail. I happen to hold exactly the opposite opinion, and to believe that most of van der Post's later books are more interesting than *In A Province*.

The difference is, fundamentally, between realism and symbolism. *In A Province* describes objects realistically and narrates events as accurately as possible. It allows physical objects to make their own impression on the reader, and narrative events to suggest their own conclusions. A page-long description near the end of the novel may illustrate this. "The police headquarters at Paulstadt" are located "at the end of a street which divides the native and coloured quarters from the houses of white people." The description goes into photographic detail: "It is a long double-storied building. Its walls are covered with a white plaster made out of a mixture of cement and well-crushed gravel . . ." Having described the building, it goes on to describe the adjoining parade-ground. Only near the end does it generalize: "Almost always one sees in this parade-ground groups of tattered and shackled natives . . . One sees almost always, too, a group of saddle horses held by a black constable, whose surroundings have made him desperately grave. As one enters the police station one finds oneself grave also." Only at the end of this long description does the author allow himself to intrude his own feelings.

In contrast to this photographic realism, the later novels use description for more symbolic purposes. A brief paragraph from the second, *The Face Beside the Fire,* describes a London evening: "Towards the west the dark, purple clouds massed over the town and drew its smoke and mists like a veil over their faces. As he stared silently the dark sky seemed to crack abruptly. The crack widened and a red and almost legendary and mythological light, a strange Wagnerian note in colour poured swiftly through it." Instead of the factual sunlight of *In A Province,* a "mythological, Wagnerian light" illuminates the darkness of the second novel. The description is symbolic, intended primarily to evoke feeling and suggest meaning.

Even the swift adventure story of *Flamingo Feather* includes many passages of description more symbolic than realistic. For instance: "Oom Pieter . . . wore his favorite wide-brimmed green hat with band of puff-adder skin . . ." He held "a seven-millimetre Mauser. . . . It was to him what a spear was to a knight in a dark and unfamiliar wood: the quintessential symbol of a lost heroic age." And as "I jumped out and went to greet him, the metal sunlight and glittering sun-beetle sound was rising up everywhere in the bush around us." The hat-band of puff-adder skin is more symbolic than picturesque, and the "seven-millimetre Mauser" is a "quientessential symbol," while the factual African sunlight of *In A Province* has become a "metal sunlight and glittering sun-beetle sound."

All these descriptive passages have been chosen to illustrate the extreme differences in style in van der Post's writings. *In A Province* is realistic, and readers who dislike symbolism prefer it: it is clearly intelligible and immediately effective. The later novels evoke feeling and suggest meaning by means of symbol and indirection, without always making things entirely clear. But at their best these novels achieve greater depth of feeling and greater complexity of meaning.

*In A Province* is divided into three separate "Books," whose chapters are numbered separately to emphasize the clear structural pattern of the novel. The first chapter, however, is properly a "prologue," which describes the spiritual illness of the hero. It ends: "To understand his mood . . . it is necessary to go back many years." The rest of Book I returns to describe the childhood and youth of van Bredepoel and to define his relationship with a Negro boy of his own age. Book II then describes the increasing conflict within the hero's mind, caused by his feeling of guilt concerning his black friend, who has now fallen afoul of the white man's law. Book III begins where the prologue to Book I ended—with the convalescence of the hero. Now he meets his black friend once again and resolves his mental conflict by determining to help him wholeheartedly. Desperately seeking to oppose the injustice of the law, he is killed by a stray bullet. The novel ends in tragedy.

*In A Province* is dominated by three major characters. The autobiographical hero stands in the middle. On the one side his black friend, Joseph Kenon, becomes gradually corrupted and finally destroyed by the white man's civilization. On the other side, Burgess, an English Communist agitator whom he meets, seeks to subvert the law which unjustly persecutes the black man. The hero is torn between his natural loyalty to family and country, and his sympathy with his black friend as well as with the Communist agitator who actively seeks to oppose injustice. But the excellence of the novel consists not so much in its major characters, or even its artistic structure, as in its vivid description of incidents in South African life, and in its minor characters. The conflict within the hero's mind is described almost entirely in terms of his experience with this outside world.

The hero's childhood is described in relationship to his sternly Calvinistic Uncle and Aunt, who contrast with his warm and skeptical tutor. His first experience in the city is related to the motherly but prejudiced proprietress of his boarding house. The ingenuous young Negro, Joseph Kenon, arrives to work at the house, and the two young men are instinctively attracted to each other. But they are kept apart by strict convention. As van Bredepoel goes about his work, the focus shifts to the Negro. Kenon is tempted by a salesman, buys a gramaphone on credit, and falls deeper and deeper into debt. He visits a brothel, which is raided by the police, but when the others all flee, the bewildered Kenon is caught. He is tried and sentenced to six months in jail. When he gets out, he has become "cheeky." He seeks employment again, but is rebuffed; and when he asks to see his old friend van Bredepoel, the landlady lies to him that the white man does not wish to see him. He drifts away and there are rumors of more serious trouble. Meanwhile the hero becomes increasingly convinced that he should have done more to help his black friend.

In Book II the focus shifts from young Kenon to "the agitators." The hero observes a street-corner meeting where a black preacher proclaims that "Christ himself was black." Some time afterwards he becomes involved in an altercation on a tram, where two white men try to force an Indian to give up his seat to a white woman. Another white man intervenes, and the hero reluctantly sides with the "nigger-kisser." This white man turns out to be a labor organizer named Burgess, and the two become friends. For the rest of Book II, van Bredepoel explores the realities of the South African racial situation with his new friend. But he also learns that Burgess is an uncompromising Communist, who stands at the opposite pole from his Negro friend Kenon. Where Book I had described the first encounter of innocence with the evil world, Book II describes the counter-attack of Communist idealism on the evil world. As van Bredepoel learns more of this communism, he becomes increasingly convinced of its evil, also. Torn between these opposites, he becomes distraught, and suffers the nervous breakdown described in the prologue to Book I.

In Book III the hero returns to a country town near the home of his childhood, in order to recuperate in peace and quiet. But he finds the opposite of peace and quiet. He meets his former friend Kenon by chance and becomes increasingly involved with him. Meanwhile he experiences the hostility of old friends of his family at "the Club." Appalled at the Fascist violence of these men, he seeks to help Kenon. But he meets Burgess again, and finds the Communist equally violent. In an impassioned argument with Burgess, he pleads for moderation. By this time, events have gone too far, and he is caught up in the violence and destroyed.

The structure of the novel is clear, and the conflict at its heart is logical. But van der Post is seldom at his best in describing the conflict of abstract ideas. Near the climax of Book III, the hero exclaims against the Communist: "Oh, curse you and your like! It's difficult, I know; but because it's difficult to bring these things about rationally and calmly, that's no excuse for not trying. I can't change my programme even for you, and that says a good deal." The language is so abstract that it loses emotional effect, and this abstraction makes the leading characters seem unreal also. Van Bredepoel's psychological illness exists in an emotional vacuum, although the physical incidents which have precipitated it are described vividly. Therefore, his sudden death at the hands of the vigilantes fails to move us deeply, although it is all-too believable. And this abstraction is finally emphasized by the last paragraph of the novel, in which the author allows himself to exhort his characters directly, like some deus-ex-machina: "Johan! Kenon! Poor, unhappy children of life, courage!"

It is not quite fair to quote these occasional abstract passages from a vividly realistic novel, because most of the narrative is concrete and fully realized. An unforgettable variety of incidents from the South African life of the 1930's succeed one another, and as the novel advances, the scenes increase in intensity. "Doc," the black preacher, orates from street-corners until he is finally shot down in a confused melee, during which the hero is also knocked down. A cocktail party, sponsored by the "Bantu-European Approach Association," portrays a mixed variety of insecure Negro males and frustrated white females, who struggle resolutely to achieve the brotherhood of man. The drunken members of the exclusive "Paulstadt Club" join in the singing of "We Are Marching to Pretoria" to suggest the groundswell of Fascist emotion. And when "van Copenhagen's commandoes" take the law into their own hands, the tragic death of van Bredepoel is predetermined.

The realistic sequence of events and the vivid interplay of

minor characters create a novel of great historical interest. The spiritual illness of its hero and his physical tragedy are fully motivated. But the depth of feeling from which he suffers, and the inner darkness of his despair, will be illuminated more fully in the later novels.

## II   The Face Beside the Fire

*The Face Beside the Fire* contrasts with *In A Province* in almost every way. In technique, it is symbolic rather than realistic. In subject matter, it describes personal relationships and inner emotion rather than political conflicts and outer action. Its hero is an artist rather than a businessman, whose "crisis" is caused by domestic alienation rather than political struggle. In structure, it lacks the formal artistry of *In A Province,* tracing instead the gradual growth of human character. It lacks unity of place, shifting from Africa to England, then back to Africa and ending in England. And it lacks unity of time: the narrative meanders from early childhood to young manhood, through one unhappy marriage and the failure of one career, to the beginning of a second marriage and career. It succeeds not by virtue of realistic art, but by the symbolic creation of mood, emotion and character.

The title is significant: it emphasizes the memory of an apparently insignificant incident in early childhood. On a family camping trip, "the daily round of schools and books fell magically away from us, and we entered a natural world which was very close to our instincts." One evening the hero was frightened by the roar of a lion, but was magically reassured by the sight of his sister's face beside the campfire, her blonde hair haloed by its reflected light. Throughout the novel, this remembered vision of childhood innocence and beauty continues to haunt him, recalling the promise of a happiness unrealized and of a natural beauty lost. Only at the novel's end can he recapture this promise in the beginning of a second marriage.

From this episode of early childhood, the story advances through six "Parts" and twenty-three "Chapters" numbered consecutively and in chronological order. Part I focuses upon the hero's mother and father, suggesting a "journey in time" into the past and describing the family conflicts which foreshadow the later conflicts within the mind of the hero. Part II describes

his "Flight" from South Africa to London and his sense of "Exile"
there. Part III focuses upon the "Crisis" of his inner life, which
results in the failure of his creative impulse and of his first marriage. In Part IV, "The Voyage," he returns to South Africa in
order to rediscover himself, and in Part V, entitled "Discovery,"
he meets his future wife on the return voyage to England. In
Part VI, the hero finally comes to terms with his own past, recovering self-confidence through self-knowledge.

If this plot seems vague and discursive, it is—considered
merely in terms of realism. If the novel were simply realistic,
this wandering action might seem footless. But the true action
is not realistic but psychological, and its true direction is inward.
The novel achieves its emotional effect of inner reality by a
variety of other means—combining narration, description, and
symbolism.

The story is narrated by a "twin" of the hero—not really a
brother, but the son of a neighboring family, born at the same
time. This narrator is described as a "normal" boy, born into a
happy family and free of those conflicts which disturb his unhappy twin. His affection for the hero, combined with his detachment, allow him to share the hero's life and also to describe
it objectively. The narrator, therefore, remains relatively unin-
volved—much like the earlier hero of In A Province before his
later, tragic involvement at the end of that novel. But if this
lack of involvement forces the narrator to remain a shadowy
character without fictional reality, it enables him to paint a kind
of stereoscopic portrait of the hero, imparting to his character a
double reality.

The hero grows up to become a painter by profession. To
characterize him more deeply, the novel first narrates his conflicts as an aspiring artist—his conflict with his ambitious mother,
who tries to force him to abandon his painting and become a
respectable lawyer, and his later conflict with society, which tries
to force him to paint only what it wants. Then the fictional narrator describes in detail a series of pictures painted by the hero,
which portray his own inner moods and ideas. To the narrative
art of the novelist is added the descriptive art of the painter.
Finally, this fictional hero is described as using the symbolic
devices of modern art to suggest the psychological nature of
his conflicts: "Two, three and even four heads on one thin neck

... were not uncommon. Many faces had two or three rows of eyes ..." By combining realistic action, pictorial description, and self-conscious symbolism, the novel achieves a remarkable characterization in depth.

If the techniques of self-conscious symbolism were dominant, the novel would seem merely "arty." More important is the less obtrusive technique by which the author suggests emotion through the realistic narration of psychologically important events. The sudden vision of the sister's face beside the campfire is emphasized by the title. Even more effective is the incident of "Black Sunday" narrated in Chapter Two. Although the symbolism is again emphasized by this title, the story can be read in purely realistic terms.

Among the Calvinistic communities of the Afrikaners, all "Sundays" were "black," of course, because all the congregations dressed in black to attend church services. But on this particular Sunday the hero's mother wore a particularly beautiful black dress, "imported straight from Paris," and richly woven so "that the material always caught the same light from a different angle and so seemed to be alive. ...There were moments when, at a distance, it took on a deep purple hue, or became a dark, twelfth-century Chinese green." Realistically described, the luminous darkness of this dress exerts a strangely hypnotic effect on the young hero. " 'Oh! It's terribly beautiful, Mother,' he answered. 'Where did you get it?' " Although the incident seems perfectly objective, the emotional disturbance caused in the young boy by this "terribly beautiful" black dress is made clear, and the ensuing blackness in his confused heart is suggested.

Before setting out for church, the mother discovers that the gold sovereign intended for their church offering has disappeared from her purse. Meanwhile the black nurse has seen the boy rummaging through the purse, and says so. But he, completely unconscious of having taken the bright gold, steadfastly denies everything. When the evidence against him becomes overwhelming, he is disgraced and whipped; nevertheless he remains passionately convinced of his own innocence, and the reader is never given more than circumstantial evidence. The boy is damned by his elders as thief and liar, although he feels himself blameless. Has the punitive spirit of the old Calvinistic religion, which forbids the beauty symbolized by the face beside the fire,

and by the shining gold sovereign, caused this blackness of his
heart, and motivated his unconscious theft and subsequent lies
and despair? Or is he truly innocent, and the whole world black?
Whatever the truth, the heart of darkness has been described
and its emotions realized in terms of realistic actions whose symbolic significance is only suggested.

Moreover, these incidents realize pictorially, and suggest symbolically, the luminous beauty of this darkness. Just as the
iridescence of the mother's black silk dress seems "terribly
beautiful," so the ambiguity of the darkness within the hero's
heart becomes terribly beautiful, in its own way.

The ambiguous beauty of this darkness is again suggested by
the painting of an African sheep-shearing. This incident (described in Chapter Eight) combines narration with pictorial
description and the suggestion of mythical symbolism. The young
narrator is working with seven black shearers inside a dark shed
while the artist-hero is sitting at the entrance painting the scene.
The first paragraph narrates the actual episode, with its contrast
of brilliant sunlight outside and dark shadow within, and the
darker bodies of the black workers. The description then focuses
on the painting itself, which is "dominated by the biggest of our
Basuto shearers . . . stripped to the waist, the silk sweat on a dark
purple skin." At his feet the sheared wool shines in a reflected
light. "As one looks at the picture one knows, instantly, how the
vision of the golden fleece must have flared up in the dark before
Jason's eyes." The actual scene and the imagined painting are
described in a rich complexity of detail which suggest the heart
of darkness, and the beauty of that darkness. The face beside the
fire, the gold sovereign, and the vision of the golden fleece all
tempt the artist to take "flight" from the African darkness on
some mythical quest. But it is the interrelation of darkness and
light which makes the light beautiful and the dark luminous.

In England the hero meets a proper English girl, years older
than he, who also paints. Because she loves and admires him,
he marries her. But he feels trapped, and his progressive alienation, both from his wife and from conventional English society,
is illustrated by a succession of his paintings, culminating in his
self-portrait, "The Exile." Meanwhile he deteriorates both as
man and as artist, until he finally deserts his wife and children and
flees to South Africa.

In the final sections of this novel, the hero has lost the impulse to paint; thus his emotions cannot be illustrated, but instead are suggested in narrative terms, in conversations with his "twin," in the description of his dreams, and through the symbolism of the storms at sea which accompany his return voyage to England. His deeply felt relationship with the woman who is to become his second wife contrasts with the stiffly formal divorce from his first wife, as darkness with light. Finally, his achieved self-confidence is described through its compelling effect on the people he meets. The novel ends with the promise of a happiness achieved after many wanderings and a strange inward quest.

In the pattern of alternation between the author's "extrovert" and "introvert" books, this novel is clearly "introvert." It narrates a story of personal discovery not unlike that of *Venture to the Interior,* but it is psychological rather than physical. It describes vividly a series of personal relationships and explores the emotions accompanying them. Beyond question, it is richer in texture and deeper in feeling than *In A Province.* But whether so thin a thread of narrative can effectively support so rich a texture of description is more doubtful. Like Thomas Mann's famous novels which re-create the mythical adventures of Joseph, its weight of symbolism may seem heavy to many readers; but for those who value psychological insight and depth of emotion, this novel ranks high.

### III   Flamingo Feather

*Flamingo Feather* (1955) is a bright novel of mystery and high adventure, the only one which can fairly be described in terms of plot—its action is more important than its characterization. Indeed, it is tempting to summarize it simply, assuming that the plot is all-important, but there is much more to it than that. *Flamingo Feather* is also a tale of *mythical* adventure, related to the African novels of H. Rider Haggard of a century ago. It is likewise a tale of quasi-oriental intrigue, recalling the antique menace of Fu Manchu, combined now with that of the Communist conspiracy. More important, it includes some of the most vivid descriptions of African life and landscape that I know. And beneath its fictional façade lies the sense of personal quest which has become the hallmark of its author. Within the tradi-

tional pattern of mystery novel, a new journey to the interior
acts out a new pattern of meaning. But the pattern of action
dominates.

The story begins with a bang—with "the sound of desperate
running, followed almost immediately by the exultant war cry
of the Amangtakwena: 'Mattalahta Buka!—At last we kill!' " This
action is immediately complicated by the fact that the narrator
is an anthropologist engaged in writing a book on the "Myth and
Mind of the Amangtakwena." The hero therefore becomes an
ideal creature who combines action with intellect. He has grown
up in the interior of Africa with his father—a famous hunter and
explorer in the tradition of Haggard's Allan Quatermain. But
this twentieth-century hero has learned from childhood to understand both the virtues and the superstitions of the native
tribes. For companion and servant he relies on Umtumwa, the
son of an Amangtakwena chief, with whom he was brought up.

The war cry with which the book begins signals the death of
an unknown Amangtakwena chieftain, who has tried to deliver
two messages—one, an envelope addressed to the hero in the
handwriting of an old friend and fellow soldier long ago captured by the Japanese in Burma, but since lost; and the other, a
flamingo feather, which announces to all Amangtakwena the
imminence of war. But why has this messenger been killed? The
clues lead to a mysterious ship, Russian-built and owned by a
local man of Mongolian descent. Without any clear knowledge
or proof of conspiracy, the hero follows the route of the ship,
ironically named "The Star of Truth," as it steams northward
toward Mozambique. Through a series of adventures and discov-
eries, he becomes convinced that the ship is running arms and
ammunition to the interior, where the Amangtakwena live. In
order to verify these suspicions, the hero leads an expedition to
explore "The Dead Land" along the coast, which consists of
swamps and forests, and is inhabited only by wild animals, ven-
omous snakes, and the tsetse fly.

Through a series of adventures described with a combination
of realistic detail and psychological terror, which would make
an ordinary safari seem like a stroll through the park, the expedition advances. They hack their way through the Great Forest
of "Duk-aduk-duk"—"Did I not know this forest was so black
and thick that in it the human heart went 'duk-aduk-duk?' " At

last they emerge on an inland bay so thickly populated by scarlet flamingoes that it seems to burn with an unearthly fire. There they find "The Star of Truth" unloading its cargo of rifles, which bands of Amangtakwena then transport inland. But they are ambushed by the enemy, and all are killed except the hero and two natives. These three escape inland, climbing toward the interior by a route which parallels that of the carriers of contraband.

Book One ends with the discovery of "The Star of Truth" by the "Flamingo Water," and the verification of the Communist conspiracy. Book Two describes the hero's journey to the interior, and his unraveling of the mysterious plot which has subverted the minds of the Amangtakwena. After another series of adventures, the hero succeeds in reaching the high interior plateau where the Amangtakwena live. There he finds his old British comrade-at-arms and fellow captive, now, incredibly, engaged in training the Communist-led Amangtakwena army. In a nightlong talk, his old friend tries to explain the strange and complex situation. After having escaped from their Japanese prison in Manchuria, the friend and another fellow prisoner had been recaptured—but this time, by the Russians. Compelled by them to teach fellow Africans at the Communist school for revolution near Tashkent, the friend had finally agreed to command this revolutionary training force in Africa, but had planned to escape from it, and to warn his friends of their danger. But the Russians had kept his comrade and fellow prisoner as a hostage, to ensure his own eventual return. Therefore he had tried to send a secret message to the hero—the bearer of which had been killed, in the first chapter of the novel. Nevertheless, he still felt that he must eventually return to Russia, to ensure his comrade's safety. Caught in the confusions of the cold war (not unlike the British captain who built "The Bridge on the River Kwai," only to destroy it later), he felt himself compelled by loyalty to his old comrade-at-arms to act the role of double agent (not unlike "the Manchurian Candidate," but conscious of his own confusion, and hoping to be able to subvert the subverter).

The climactic action of the novel now takes place among the native Amangtakwena. Their tribal Council proves to be as divided and confused in its loyalties as the whites. One faction remains loyal to the British Protectorate but the other, eager for independence and angered at the insensitive administration

of the British, plans sabotage and eventual revolution. Into this
Council, which is debating the issue, the hero steps. Discarding
his rifle, he comes armed only with his recently acquired knowledge of the conspiracy and with his lifelong knowledge of the
"Myth and Mind of the Amangtakwena."

Thus the climax of this fast-moving novel of mystery and adventure results—not in physical violence, but in a strange melodrama of the mind. Knowing intimately the ways of the tribe,
the hero tempts the leaders of the rebellious faction into revealing their treachery—not to any British administration, but to their
own chiefs and medicine men. Through a series of subtle maneu-
vers, he suggests how the Communist-inspired rebels have subverted the ancient authority of their own tribe. They have pre-
ferred the alien logic of communism to the traditional wisdom
of their own people.

By these non-violent methods of persuasion, the rebellious faction of the Amangtakwena is dramatically discredited. The leaders of the conspiracy are condemned to death by their own
people, and destroyed. The hero blows up the secret store of
contraband ammunition stacked in a secluded mountain cave,
and the native Communist conspiracy, whose very existence had
been unknown to the bumbling British administrators, is erased
from the earth as if it had never been. By virtue of his courage
and his knowledge of primitive Africa, the hero has achieved
victory.

Thus far *Flamingo Feather* follows the traditional course of
the novel of mystery and adventure to its victorious conclusion.
But the novel also suggests a new pattern of meaning. At its end,
the hero's old comrade-at-arms, who has unwillingly been training the Communist army of the Amangtakwena, returns sadly
to Russia, compelled by loyalty to his other comrade-at-arms
whom they hold hostage. He remains a prisoner of the confusions of the cold war. At the end, also, the hero tells the British
administrators of this conspiracy, hoping to impress them with
the need of a more enlightened policy toward the natives. They
are impressed, instead, with the treachery of the natives and the
need for more repressive measures: they, too, have become prisoners of the cold war. The hero remains alone, both in his victory, and in his understanding of the causes of the conflict.

The fault of *Flamingo Feather* lies, I think, in the author's attempt to make this tale of high adventure bear too heavy a weight of moral meaning. The complicated story of the British prisoner-of-war forced by the Communists to act as their agent in Africa is strange enough, but acceptable for purposes of melodrama. But it is much too incredible for purposes of analysis. The excellence of the novel lies in the excitement of its plot, which holds the reader in suspense to the end, and even more in its descriptions of the wildness of Africa, both animal and human. The "flamingo feather" of the title symbolizes not only the mysterious message explained at the beginning of the novel but also the wild life which, perhaps, is the true hero of the book. Consider this description of a bull elephant as it first catches the scent of human intruders:

His long trunk hung straight down in front of him with a heavy, sagging immobility until it began to curl over ever so faintly at the outermost tip and to glisten with a light rhododendron pinkness as it began to search the air in our direction. I couldn't help smiling at the expression which then came over that monumental face as the heavy skin of his great trunk, with a wonderful butterfly flutter, puckered like the nose of a baby about to sneeze.

These two sentences not only re-create the elephant for the visual imagination but also realize the moral innocence of the African wild.

## IV   The Seed and the Sower

*The Seed and the Sower* (1963) is one of the most imaginative of the author's books, but at the same time one of the least popular. Some readers believe it one of his best; others actively dislike it. To account for such difference of opinion, something more than literary criticism is needed. The novel explores fundamental issues of religion and human psychology, narrating actions and suggesting interpretations which disturb many people. But its originality of conception and frequent brilliance of execution may well outweigh its occasional failures.

Actually, *The Seed and the Sower* is not strictly a novel; it is a collection of three separate novellas, or long short stories, written at different times but bound together by a common theme and cast of characters. The narrator and his former comrade-at-arms, John Lawrence, recall their wartime experiences in the course of a Christmas weekend, while the narrator's wife occasionally listens and questions. The first novella (originally published in 1952 as "A Bar of Shadow") consists of a dialogue between the narrator and John Lawrence, recalling their experiences in a Japanese prison camp, and after. The second story, which is much more complex, begins and ends with dialogue, but consists chiefly of a long "autobiography" written in prison by a third comrade, who was executed by the Japanese. The third story is simpler, consisting of the account by John Lawrence of his love affair with a Dutch girl just before his capture by the Japanese.

These three novellas explore elemental aspects of the conflicting emotions of hatred and love engendered by war. They are so unequal, both in scope and in quality, that they sometimes seem not to belong together. The first focuses sharply on the relationship of mixed hatred and respect between a Japanese jailor and his captive, John Lawrence. The second, larger in scope and more ambitious in conception, describes a second conflict between a second Japanese jailor and a South African officer. But this conflict of wartime enemies is both introduced and counterpointed by an earlier conflict of siblings—between the South African and his younger brother, before the war. Finally, the double conflict leads the South African to choose a voluntary martyrdom at the hands of the Japanese. This complex tale with its Biblical parallels—to the conflict of Cain and Abel, and to the crucifixion—becomes so fascinating that, after it, the third story of a simple love affair in the shadow of war seems flat and unreal. Such inequality may well have contributed to the imperfect success of the book as a whole.

The excellence of the book lies in the combination of narrative, symbol, and interpretation by which it communicates both physical excitement and psychological meaning. The title of the first novella, "A Bar of Shadow," suggests not only the actual shadow of the prison bars but also the psychological shadow of the imprisoning hatred engendered by the war. The fictional re-creation of this double darkness results in a story of great emotional power and fascination. "A Bar of Shadow" incarnates this double physical and psychological darkness in the character of the Japanese jailor, Hara. An embodiment of all the inscrutable cruelty which allied prisoners of war had experienced as evil at the hands of their oriental captors, Hara is re-created in the conversations of the narrator and John Lawrence. Simultaneously, his character is examined and explained by Lawrence, in the light of his extensive knowledge of Japanese customs, both before the war and after. Hara, he says, embodied "the living myth ... the personification of the intense, inner vision which, far down in their consciousness, keeps the Japanese people together and shapes and compels their thinking and behaviour." He was a worshiper of the moon-goddess, and of the dark, instinctual self to which Orientals have always given more value than Occidentals. Thus understood, Hara was not evil, but compelled by a religious psychology alien to the West. His cruelty might therefore be forgiven, and his selfless devotion to his religion even admired, if seen from his own point of view. At the end, Lawrence tells of his futile effort to save Hara from execution by a War Crimes Tribunal. "It seemed to me just as wrong for us now to condemn Hara under a law which had never been his, of which he had never heard, as he and his masters had been to punish and kill us for transgressions of the code of Japan that was not ours."

The meaning is clear and the interpretation convincing, but the highest quality of the novella lies in its vivid narration of the wartime incidents which have motivated the interpretation and which illustrate its meaning. These incidents are chosen not only to illustrate the dark cruelty of Hara but also to suggest his occasional human kindness. Compelled by his own religious myth, he also appreciated the religious myths of his captives, and typically ordered them one December to celebrate the feast of "Fazeru Kurīsumasu." But when they failed to understand his Japanese pronunciation of "Father Christmas," he grew purple with anger; and when a captive Chinese officer failed to acknowledge this alien religious ritual, Hara beat the man violently. "Tonight I am Fazeru Kurīsumasu!" he proclaimed. This grotesque incident suddenly illuminates the universality of that religious fanaticism which often lies at the heart of human darkness.

"A Bar of Shadow" succeeds brilliantly in describing the heart of darkness within the body and soul of the enemy. But the second and central story of *The Seed and the Sower* is even more ambitious in its attempt to describe the heart of darkness within the human soul itself—the aboriginal sinfulness which motivates all human hatred and war, and which exists within the soul of comrade and brother as well. To introduce this story, the narrator and John Lawrence recall the dark moods which characterized their former South African comrade, "Straffer Jack" Celliers. Lawrence comments: "I always had a feeling he'd never come through alive." And the character of Celliers is developed by the long autobiography which he composed in their Japanese prison camp shortly before his execution. This autobiography begins: "I had a brother once and I betrayed him." It then traces the ambivalent relationship between the brilliant, blond Jacques Celliers and his ill-formed, dark, younger brother. The first half explores their early life together and illuminates the confused mixture of brotherly love and suppressed hatred which led to this "betrayal." The second half describes the consequent sense of guilt which drove "Straffer Jack" to volunteer for the most dangerous missions of the war and eventually to choose martyrdom at the hands of the Japanese.

The conflict between the blond and the dark brothers is narrated in three vivid episodes. First the young Jacques defends his ill-favored brother against childhood tormentors and wins the plaudits of his friends. Yet he begins to despise his brother because of it. Later, he refuses to protect his brother from some sadistic hazing at their preparatory school, only to be overcome by a sense of guilt. Finally, he shoots a malformed buck, which he symbolically identifies with his brother, rather than one of the handsome leaders of the herd. And his brother's silent reproach further increases his sense of guilt. When World War II is declared, he rushes off to volunteer.

The second half of the autobiography narrates the hero's exploits as commando in North Africa leading to his choice as commander of a school of guerrilla warfare established in Palestine. But in the Holy Land he meets a German monk who had formerly been an ace in World War I. Conversing with him, he suddenly sees a vision of the violence which stretches back through history to the crucifixion. Suffering a kind of religious conversion, he obtains leave to fly home to South Africa, where he makes his peace with his younger brother. Returning to duty, he fights on, until his capture by the Japanese. But when they are preparing one of their exemplary executions, Celliers suddenly acts to bring down their violence upon his own head, so that he is killed instead of the intended victims.

The episodes of the conflict between the two brothers are narrated with vivid realism, as are the episodes of commando warfare and of calculated Japanese terrorism. Most vividly, the strange sequence of acts by which the hero draws down punishment in order to save his comrades is narrated with convincing realism. Yet as the autobiographical narrative unfolds, it becomes increasingly clear that the story is more fable than fact. The two brothers become the two complementary halves of an archetypal human self, rather than separate individuals. And the panoramic odyssey of the hero from childhood in the interior of Africa, to conversion in the Holy Land, to voluntary martyrdom in the Far East, becomes a parable of the historic odyssey of civilized man, with its strange mixture of violent tragedy and spiritual transcendence.

This combination of vivid realism and imaginative symbolism contributes to the fascination and power of the story. But it also creates an ambivalence which occasionally becomes disturbing. The mixed emotions of love and hate are, of course, disturbing in themselves. These are well objectified in the story: Celliers emphasizes that "from an early age most people found my looks disturbing." And when he consciously chooses martyrdom, his own comrades feel a strong sense of revulsion: " 'My God! What a bastard!' an Australian infantry officer behind me exclaimed bitterly." The ambivalence of all human emotion is realized and described objectively.

Sometimes, however, the narrative labors under too heavy a weight of symbolism. The dark brother becomes too clear an incarnation of the heart of darkness: "His skin was a Mediterranean olive and his eyes ... were wide and of an intense radiant blackness." The violent emotions of the story, which are first described and narrated, are later symbolized by the parallel descriptions of violent storms and natural phenomena. Narrative events which could be allowed to produce their own effects are too often underlined, as it were, either symbolically, or explicitly. And the final story of the book is rendered almost unreal by this self-conscious striving for explicit meaning.

*The Seed and the Sower* is brilliant but uneven. It is original, powerfully imaginative, and often illuminating. But it is also disturbing, oversymbolic, and often flawed. Whether the reader admires it or rejects it will depend primarily on his own temperament and sense of literary values. This reader admires it greatly.

## V   The Hunter and the Whale

*The Hunter and the Whale* is the longest of the author's novels, and probably the best: it is the largest in scope, the richest in detail, and the most vivid in characterization. It is unlike any of his earlier novels, although it develops elements of each; it returns to *In A Province* for its conscious form, its realistic style, and its African locale; it develops the symbolism of *The Face Beside the Fire*, but without the self-consciousness of the earlier novel; it introduces an international cast of characters, like *The Seed and the Sower*, including representatives of different nations and races; and although it is subtitled "A Tale of Africa," much of its action takes place on the high seas. It owes least to the melodramatic excitement of *Flamingo Feather*.

In form this novel follows the earlier pattern of *In A Province*. The first chapter begins "*in medias res*," when the young hero has already served three years on a Norwegian whaler. As in the earlier novel, he now faces a crisis whose nature he can only dimly understand. The second chapter then returns to a time "three years before," when the narrator was only fourteen. Chapters Two to Ten describe in a leisurely manner the events of these earlier years which have led up to the present crisis. Chapter Eleven returns to "that Saturday evening at the beginning of my fourth whaling season." A new character has appeared on the scene—a veteran elephant hunter who has come from the interior to the ocean seeking bigger game. This strange man persuades the captain of the whaler to join in a new hunt for the greatest game that exists—the sperm whale. The last three chapters lead swiftly to the final catastrophe, with its unique ending.

As this brief summary suggests, the novel is divided sharply into two parts. The first ten chapters tell of the young hero's initiation into the world—a world of work among men, and of adventure on the high seas. This first part is dominated by the autobiographical character of the young narrator, gradually growing to maturity both in experience and in wisdom. The last four chapters then tell of the whalers' hunt for the great sperm whale nicknamed "*L'Empereur*," or "Caesar." This second part is dominated by twin characters: that of Thor Larsen, the dour Norwegian captain who has commanded the ship from the beginning, and that of Herklaas (Hercules) de la Buschagne, the elephant hunter whose daemonic purpose now persuades the captain to engage in the hunt for leviathan, which he had long dreamed of but never before actually attempted.

This division into two parts is, however, only formal. Chapter Two is entitled simply, "Captain." The young hero's first meeting with Thor Larsen is recounted in great detail; the Captain is characterized both in action and in abstract description. "He struck me at once as a person strangely dark. . . . It was a blackness, moreover, that owed nothing to the color of hair or skin. . . . Ibsen, Strindberg and even the fairy tales of Hans Andersen are charged for me with a frightening element of darkness." The Norse captain is then characterized by the Zulu butler as having "the eyes of a *nyanga*—a witch doctor." And soon this characterization is realized in action: "He seized my arm in his broad hand, squeezed it, and a look came into his eye, which, remembering the butler's description of it, might have been that of a sorcerer acknowledging a chosen apprentice." The symbolic pattern is thus defined, with its prediction of future catastrophe; but the concrete narrative has seemed so naturalistic that the young hero continues to dominate the first half of the novel.

The character of this autobiographical hero soon achieves an objective reality greater than that of van der Post's other novels. Good autobiography requires perspective, and a distance of forty years separates the mature author of this novel from his boyhood hero. The author had sailed on whaling voyages from "Port Natal" at the ages of seventeen and eighteen, and he had narrated the factual outlines of these in his early article written in Afrikaans, *"Nimrods van die See."* All the concrete detail of *The Hunter and the Whale* is as autobiographically authentic as that of Melville's whaling novels, because both young authors had experienced and observed it. But whereas Melville's autobiographical narrator pales progressively into abstraction with the increasing symbolism of his whaling novels, until the narrator of *Moby Dick* becomes only a mouthpiece for the author, the young narrator of *The Hunter and the Whale* becomes its most fully realized character. His reality, moreover is both naturalistic and symbolic.

When the young hero first meets the Captain, "The scene presented itself to me rather like some painting by a 'primitive,'... innocent like that of man's in the Garden before the Fall." His relationships with the Zulu butler and the black stoker, Mlangeni, remain equally "innocent" and natural; but their very naturalness arouses the enmity of the representative of the ship's owner, and the jealousy of the Captain. He suffers from this enmity, but his natural skill and sharpness of vision earn him the job of "spotter" on the whaler. Scornfully nicknamed "Peter-Bright-Eye" at first, he soon becomes simply "Eyes." Progressively rejected by the aristocratic owner's representative and his spoiled son, he is progressively accepted by the democratic crew. A closely knit friendship gradually develops between four of its oddly assorted members—the young hero, two Norwegian sailors, and the Zulu stoker.

The adolescent hero experiences "the moment of [his] own private and personal birth" when he feels himself fully accepted into this international community of the sea. The Norwegian cook, Leif, slowly tutors him in the lore of whaling—for Leif is explorer both of the world of work and the world of meaning. And the Norwegian helmsman, "Gorgeous" (a corruption of Georghius) Grieg (a fifth cousin of the composer), is a dreamer in exile, who plays classical music endlessly on his gramophone. But Leif the explorer of knowledge and Gorgeous the lover of culture remain essentially foreigners, who educate the hero in the lore of the sea and the historic culture of Europe. It is the Zulu stoker, Mlangeni, who most influences him: "Much as I was drawn to Leif, I had experienced immediately a sense of kinship with Mlangeni, the kinship which comes alive in the children of Africa whatever their colour when they are among foreigners." This strangely international and interracial foursome make the nucleus of the democratic crew.

The character of Mlangeni (the Captain pronounces it "Langenay") is central to the "Tale of Africa." He is personal friend and senior adviser to the young hero, and he is also representative of the black races of Africa—both protector of youthful innocence, and protected by the young hero's civilized experience. A chosen leader of his people in their quest for equality in a larger world (symbolized by the sea), he is also an individual character wholly realized in action and speech. On the personal level, his role is suggested by the title of Chapter Six: *"Tutaka! Nkosan, Tutaka!"*—"Grow! Little Prince, Grow!" On the racial level his role is realized in what the hero describes as "the strangest of processions." One morning on a secluded beach Mlangeni leads a group of Zulu countrymen to a kind of ritual baptism in the ocean, explaining that "it was time to renounce the ancient fear of the sea and lead his people back to the great water. This was the way to add the white man's knowledge to their own."

The young hero gradually achieves full maturity by assuming the responsibility for the education of Mlangeni in the ways of civilization. He acts as translator and mediator between the stoker and the rest of the crew. Then, when a new and bigoted member of the crew attempts to "frame" Mlangeni, he manages to circumvent the treachery. Finally, when Mlangeni feels drawn to desert the ship in order to assume leadership of his country-men during a racial riot on shore, the hero persuades the Captain to keep the stoker below deck away from temptation. Mean-while Mlangeni interprets signs of trouble for his young friend and particularly warns of impending catastrophe when the two *"iziyanga,"* or medicine men, get together. Through the complex interrelationship of white boy and black man, the novel devel-ops its "Tale of Africa."

The second part of the novel begins with the sudden arrival of the veteran elephant hunter, Herklaas de la Buschagne, nick-named "One-Bullet." Because this old Afrikaner cannot speak much English, the young hero translates his story for the Cap-tain—and for the reader. De la Buschagne tells of his lifelong hunt for the mammoth elephant named "Sway-Back," and ex-plains how one day "it occurred to him that he had been hunting the wrong quarry. He should have been seeking not the greatest animal on earth but the greatest animal life had ever produced. And that, he knew, was the whale." Therefore he has come to the famous Captain Larsen asking help in his hunt for "Caesar," the great sperm whale.

The long story of "One-Bullet and Sway-Back" is narrated in realistic detail against a rich background of African life and legend. It introduces the second part of the book, with its uni-versal story of the hunting of the great sperm whale on the high seas and naturalizes it as "A Tale of Africa." Moreover, it develops effectively the symbolic theme of the hunting of leviathan, suggested by the Book of Job, in terms appropriate to the character of de la Buschagne, who is described as a Bible-quoting Afrikaner of the old school. Nevertheless, this sudden introduction of a fabulous story in the midst of an effectively realistic novel seems only to emphasize the conscious idea behind it, at the expense of all that has gone before. Where the character of Captain Larsen has been realized gradually in naturalistic narrative of direct action, with all his mixture of human pride and frailty, the story of de la Buschagne is told in indirect dialogue, and his wholly daemonic character remains somewhat too inhuman and too abstract. This seems the weakest part of the novel.

But the final chapter achieves magnificence. It tells the story of the whaler's voyage into the eye of the storm in quest of the great sperm whale, reaching its climax in the description of the harpooning of "Caesar" by the two human Caesars—Captain Larsen and de la Buschagne. Combining narrative realism with an unobtrusive naturalistic symbolism, this contains some of van der Post's finest writing. Consider the paragraph describing the first surfacing of "Caesar" from the depths of the sea:

This time everyone in the ship saw its blow and the *Kurt Hansen*, already leaping forward at full speed from my first shout, was fast closing the narrow gap between Caesar and ourselves. But so quickly was the swell rushing, like a wave of crude oil, towards us and blocking the view below, that I doubt if anyone saw what I saw. I saw Caesar's great square battering head, his jaws slightly parted and the corner of his long mouth upturned as if in a grin of triumph. His dreadnought head seemed covered, as I thought, with giant seaweed from the jungle in the ocean valley from which he had just come. But when, instantly, I put the ship's glasses on him I saw that they were long writhing tentacles trying to get a hold, or purchase on that platinum crown of Caesar's. They failed, and during the seconds when I had Caesar in the focus of the glasses I saw them being sucked like some kind of deep-sea spaghetti into his mouth. I had no doubt that we had found Caesar in his moment of victory devouring a great cephalopod of evil for his high tea.

In this one memorable image the Caesarism of nature is both realized and symbolized. The sperm whale feasts upon the octopus while the human hunters rush toward their kill.

The final catastrophe is narrated with equal skill. The harpoon strikes home, but Caesar dives with such sudden power that the ship is pulled sideways, and simultaneously a great wall of water strikes it. From their high place both the Captain and de la Buschagne are swept overboard into the sea. The ship rights itself briefly, and the helmsman severs the harpoon line with one desperate stroke of an ax. Suddenly freed of her three "Caesars"—whale, Captain, and elephant hunter—the ship with her captainless crew limps home.

This novel inevitably challenges comparison with *Moby Dick*. Both novels narrate the hunting of a great sperm whale in full realistic detail but with overtones of symbolic meaning. Both whaling ships are commanded by daemon-driven captains, and both crews include representatives of different races and nationalities. Both novels move slowly, interrupted by frequent philosophical digressions and complicated by minor incidents and events. Fundamentally, both tell the story of Leviathan.

Yet although *Moby Dick* has become enthroned as a major classic, the comparison is not wholly onesided. On the level of realism, *The Hunter and the Whale* describes the techniques of modern whaling as fully as *Moby Dick* described those of the century before. Where *Moby Dick* concentrated this realistic detail awkwardly in its central section, *The Hunter* distributes it better throughout the story, with the result that the narrative moves more smoothly. In spite of interruptions and complications, *The Hunter* makes easy reading. Both novels include passages of swift narration and magnificent description. But in form and organization of detail, *The Hunter* is better planned.

On the level of symbolism, both novels are effective, for both authors are masters of the art. But the unique greatness of *Moby Dick* derives from the deeply subconscious nature of its symbolism, whose meanings can never be fully defined, nor whose interest exhausted. Whether the symbolic meaning of *The Hunter* may prove equally deep, only time can tell. But its complication of the elephant hunter, suddenly introduced late in the story, seems somewhat artificial. And the device by which the Captain and the elephant hunter are both swept overboard in the very moment of their victory over "Caesar," although narrated flawlessly, seems somewhat unlikely. It is as though van der Post had sought to exorcise the Caesarism of the world by one great gesture: only the daemon-driven captains are destroyed, while the ship with its crew returns to port. It seems almost as though Emerson had imagined a new ending for *Moby Dick*.

Yet although the ending of *The Hunter* is not fully tragic, it is not fully optimistic either. The story ends with an inquiry into the causes of the disaster, during which the owner's representative seeks to fix blame on the young hero. This irrational hostility of the aristocratic representative of power toward the natural democrat persists in acute form. Caesarism has not been destroyed with the Caesars; yet something intangible has been accomplished, for the master of the inquiry, named Harry England, warmly defends the young hero and exonerates him from all guilt. The climate of opinion has changed, and the natural democrat has been accepted by the new society. Alienated from his own people, he has found his home in the larger world.

# CHAPTER 6

# *Myth and Meaning: "and Beyond."*

ALL the books of Laurens van der Post are to some degree autobiographical. Some, like *A View of All the Russias*, use autobiography simply as a framework. Others, like *Venture to the Interior*, use it more subtly for purposes of association and suggestion, including memories and dreams together with external events. *The Dark Eye in Africa* recalls a variety of incidents to illustrate the author's ideas. And of course the novels convert it by symbolic means into the materials of fiction. But very few of these autobiographical materials are used more than once. The single incident, whose repetition calls attention to its importance, is that of the Sudanese camel-drivers in the Abyssinian campaign at the beginning of World War II.

Typically, the author first recalls this incident while meeting an old friend and colleague: the pilot of the plane now carrying him on his "Venture to the Interior" proves to be the same South African who had first managed to land supplies for his commandos behind the Italian lines nine years before. "From that day onwards, all of us who were with Dan Sandford and Orde Wingate had an assured source of supply from the air. Our long and precarious supply line depending on camels whose route one could have followed blindfold for hundreds of miles, going only by the stink of the dead animals, could at last be closed."

The following day of his "Venture to the Interior" he is reminded of the Sudanese camel-drivers of this Abyssinian campaign by the faces of some natives whom he observes on the streets of Khartoum:

I thought of my Sudanese camel-men in the war. I had been given very definite orders that when I got through into Abyssinia and reached the great Gojjam escarpment, I was to send back at once to the Sudan my camels and camel-men, who were civilians from Kor-

131

dofan. I was told that at the foot of the mountains I would find mules
and Abyssinian muleteers to take over my loads and go on with me.
However, things turned out otherwise. When we reached the foot of
the mountains we found neither mules nor muleteers. Furthermore
our arms and supplies were desperately needed. We decided to dis-
obey orders and to take the camels on into the mountains. As the
camel-men were all civilians and I could not order them to go on,
I asked for volunteers.

By that time they had all done as much, if not more, than they had
ever contracted to do. A number of them were ill with malaria, dysentery and tropical ulcers; others had sores and festering feet. And
worst of all, up there in the foothills they were miserable with cold
at night. Some had pneumonia, some had bronchitis and all had colds
and coughs. None of them had anything to wear but thin cotton
smocks torn and tattered on the journey.

They were in such a state, in fact, that some of my European officers protested against my decision to take them on. An officer with
me, who was killed a week later by an Italian bullet, felt so strongly
about it that he refused to interpret for me. Nevertheless I had called
all the Sheiks to my tent where we talked it over frankly and at great
length. After many hours the oldest of them suddenly spoke up
firmly: "Effendi," he said, "we have come a long way with you. We
are far from our homes and we have done all that we promised to do.
We are sick; we are cold; our feet are tired and full of sores. But I
am older than any of these people here. I can remember what it used
to be like before the Government came. If the Government wants us
to go on, we will go on." This phrase, "Before the Government came,"
stuck in my mind. I found the phrase most significant. Subsequently
I came across it over and over again.

This is vivid autobiographical writing: it narrates the concrete
incidents of an exciting adventure occurring in a strange country
during a historic campaign. Most of van der Post's autobiographical writing is equally vivid and concrete. But it is much more.
This incident is remembered during the course of his later flight to
the interior, in association with meeting a friend and observing
some native Sudanese. The recollection of this incident focuses,
not upon the excitement of wartime adventure, but upon the
comradeship of wartime experience and upon the loyalty of the
native camel-drivers. And at the end the author repeats the significant phrase, "before the Government came," in order to emphasize this unforced loyalty to an alien command.

In *The Dark Eye in Africa,* he retells this same incident in equally vivid detail. But this time his purpose is not the recollection of emotion, but rather the illustration of idea. The central theme of *The Dark Eye* is the emphatic contrast between the extraordinary friendliness of African natives toward European government at first, and their dark hatred in later times. In order to prove this point: "Allow me to give you one more instance of what I meant." After retelling the Abyssinian incident, he now generalizes upon the phrase, "before the Government came." He concludes with a final appeal to autobiography: "I could give you many other examples drawn from my own experience of life in rural Africa."

The repetition of this incident illustrates the different uses of autobiography in his books. But beyond the obvious uses for narrative and philosophical purposes, this incident also suggests unobtrusively the difference between the character of the author and of his associates. After detailing vividly the sufferings of the Sudanese, he records that "some of my European officers protested against my decision to take them on." And "one felt so strongly about it that he refused to interpret for me." "Nevertheless," in spite of opposition from colleagues, and in spite of his own ignorance of the language, he spoke to the sheiks so persuasively that they volunteered for difficult service beyond the call of duty. Like Lawrence of Arabia, he understood the appeal of danger to the native mind, and the appeal of personal example beyond verbal persuasion. Like T. E. Lawrence, but unlike most other Europeans, he was able to identify effectively with people of different races and more primitive cultures than his own.

## I  *"Laurens of Abyssinia"*

The autobiographical nature of van der Post's writing, the dangerous and often exotic nature of the events described, and finally the extraordinary personality revealed both by the writing and the events, all suggest comparison with the life and writing of Lawrence of Arabia. An almost legendary aura attaches to both men. Each became a colonel in the British army in a world war; each led a dangerous campaign through a savage country; and each succeeded by virtue of his deep understanding of, and fellowship with, the natives. Each was captured, and each subjected to torture by the enemy; but each survived to write of his adventures after the war. This comparison has been suggested by others, but long before van der Post had begun writing these books, the comparison had been suggested by his own colleagues. During the war his fellow officers had nicknamed him "Laurens of Abyssinia."

This nickname, acquired during the Abyssinian campaign which his books have described so vividly, may suggest the central significance both of the man and of his books. With Lawrence of Arabia, he stands as the latest of a long line of English warrior-adventurers who have also been men of letters. Beginning with Sir Walter Raleigh and the early Elizabethan explorers, these men have narrated their adventures in unexplored lands and have celebrated their contacts with savage peoples. At first merely "histories" of external exploits, their books of exploration have increasingly become stories of cultural discovery, narrating the inner experiences of living with savage peoples of alien lands. Beginning in the early nineteenth century with Sir Richard Burton, this literature has focused upon Asia and Africa, and upon the exotic and often erotic customs of the most savage and un-English of these cultures. In the late nineteenth century Charles M. Doughty both lived and wrote his *Travels in Arabia Deserta*, describing vividly his years of sharing the life of the native Arabs to the point of actual identification with them. And in the early twentieth century T. E. Lawrence actually became "Lawrence of Arabia," both in fact and in literary imagination.

Laurens van der Post, nicknamed "Laurens of Abyssinia," is the latest of this long line of English explorer-authors who have progressively chronicled and celebrated the meeting of European civilization with American, Asian, and African savagery. Like all these he has been first of all an actor and after that an author. But because he is the latest of this long line, he has most easily understood and most fully described the savage cultures among which he has lived. And because—unlike all these English explorers before him—he himself was born in the interior of that Africa which he has described, he has both lived and written of it from within. Unlike Lawrence of Arabia, he has never needed to "un-selve" himself in order to understand and identify with these alien and uncivilized cultures.

Indeed, the differences between Lawrence of Arabia and Laurens van der Post are as significant as their similarities. "A man who gives himself to be a possession of aliens leads a Yahoo life, having bartered his soul to a brute-master,"[1] wrote T. E. Lawrence.

In my case, the effort of these years to live in the dress of Arabs, and to imitate their mental foundation, quitted me of my English self, and let me look at the West and its conventions with new eyes: they destroyed it all for me.

But van der Post has not dressed in alien clothes, nor sought to imitate "brute" customs: when he has looked at alien conventions with new eyes, they have not destroyed his sense of identity. "Sometimes," continued Lawrence, "[my two] selves would converse in the void; and then madness was very near, as I believe it would be near the man who could see things through the veils at once of two customs, two educations, two environments."[1] But Laurens van der Post has seen things through the veils of different customs and educations all his life without loss of identity, because he has never identified himself exclusively with his civilized European heritage.

Indeed, the nickname "Laurens of Abyssinia" seems something of a misnomer, because van der Post has never been identified with Abyssinia as has Lawrence with Arabia. When he led this expedition from the Sudan in World War II, he had never been to Abyssinia and had never seen a camel. He had been chosen for the task because of his experience and general knowledge of Africa. The Abyssinian campaign lasted less than a year, and when it ended he was sent on to North Africa, and later Indonesia. He returned to Addis Ababa only in 1966, to help celebrate the twenty-fifth anniversary of the Emperor's triumphal return to his capital. He was "of Abyssinia" only briefly, and almost by an accident of history.

Yet symbolically, Laurens van der Post was, and is, "of Abyssinia." For Abyssinia has always been a legendary country, where civilization and savagery have often met. Just as "Arabia" has symbolized the meeting of East and West, of Asia and Europe, so Abyssinia symbolizes the meeting of North and South, of Eurasia and Africa. From Abyssinia the legendary Queen of Sheba journeyed to King Solomon's court. Dr. Johnson's *Rasselas*,

*Prince of Abyssinia* (1759) somewhat vaguely imagines it as a philosophers' paradise. And historically, this land has been the only Christian country of Africa. Yet the very wildness of the country has isolated it from the progress of civilization, just as its monasteries have remained isolated near the sources of the Blue Nile, undiscovered until recent times. Christianity and civilization have survived here mostly in myth. And this myth of a legendary civilization in Africa suggested the timeless white queen of H. Rider Haggard's novels, who rules over her subjects in the dark interior, and the white goddess of the African rock paintings which van der Post has so eloquently described. But this legendary civilization has also persisted as fact: he has told of meeting a group of Abyssinian natives, "with garlands of wild flowers round their necks, marching toward me ... playing on pipes exactly like the Pipes of Pan, which I had only known from Greek vases." To this Abyssinia of half-legend and half-history, half-civilization and half-savagery, where primitive Christianity has mingled with the gods of Grecian antiquity in the wild interior of Africa, Laurens van der Post symbolically belongs.

But just as he is not "of Abyssinia" (as T. E. Lawrence was "of Arabia"), so only a part of him belongs to Abyssinia even in the symbolic sense. For "Laurens" is only his first name, and the whole purpose of the nickname was half-humorous—the invention of fellow soldiers, intended as much for "kidding" as for characterization. "Van der Post" does not belong to Abyssinia, but to South Africa and to England.

Yet Laurens van der Post (unlike T. E. Lawrence, whose first names have been forgotten) may be more truly characterized by his informal first name than by his official last name. Although his Abyssinian nickname was given half in jest, "Laurens" suggests his inner nature and the significance of his career, both in actual fact and in literary imagination. The natural informality of life in all the recently settled and civilized countries of the modern world has found historic expression in their common use of first names. In nineteenth-century America, for instance, Walter Whitman chose the nickname "Walt" to characterize his ideal, poetic American "self"; and increasingly in American practice first names have been used to suggest the friendly informality of our national life. The same informality has resulted in the same usage in South Africa. And throughout his life van der

Post has been known by his first name to a much larger and more varied group of friends and acquaintances, both in Africa and throughout the world, than any native-born Englishman. Where T. E. Lawrence belonged to Arabia by his last name only, "Laurens" belongs to Abyssinia and to all the countries of the modern world more by informal association than by last name.

## II  *Personae and Personality*

Even if "Laurens" was "of Abyssinia" only briefly, symbolically, and informally, "Lawrence" actually became his last name in a very real sense two years later in Indonesia. In his Japanese prisoner-of-war camp in Java he adopted the nom de plume of "John Lawrence" to use in editing a prison newsletter and in organizing other prison activities. And many years later still, "John Lawrence" became the name of one of his autobiographical characters in *The Seed and the Sower*. This transformation of the informal "Laurens" into the pseudonymous "John Lawrence," and finally into the fictional John Lawrence of the novel, may suggest the complex interrelationship of historic fact and literary imagination which characterizes both the author and his books. And it may suggest how fact and fiction have gradually fused to create the vivid auctorial personality which dominates all his books.

The first quality of this personality is its actual—and active—reality. This relates him to the actual soldier, "Lawrence of Arabia," and to the actual author-explorers of Elizabethan times. And it is this active reality which he himself most values in literature. Recognizing the parallel between T. E. Lawrence and himself, and describing how "I was nicknamed 'Laurens of Abyssinia,'" he has supposed that "this may be due to the fact that writing has never seemed to me to be something just of commitment of meaning to pen and paper. It seems to me also something which has to be lived. The writer, it seems to me, short of physical disabilities which may prevent him, should also be a man of action, just as most of the great Elizabethans—even John Donne—were."[2] Although he had begun his auctorial career as writer of fiction, he had first realized his full powers and recognized his true "commitment" during the intensely active years of the war. Since then all his books have celebrated the active experiences from which literary "meaning" has gradually emerged.

This intense commitment to the life of action, and this total belief in the value—and even the necessity—of action to the man of letters, relates him to T. E. Lawrence and distinguishes all his writing since the war. It contributes to the intense conviction of personal reality which this writing communicates. But it also differentiates his writing from that of many men of letters who have taken comparatively little part in the active life of the world. Even Walt Whitman, for instance, whose intense realization of an auctorial personality resembles his in many ways, created "Myself" as much out of literary imagination as actual fact. Among men of letters van der Post stands almost unique in the degree to which actual experience dominates fictional imagination in the realization of his literary myth.

But the quality which most differentiates him from T. E. Lawrence—and from all those explorers and men of action who have transformed their actual experiences into literature—is the extraordinary variety of his experiences, and the extraordinary multiplicity of his relationships with all sorts of people in all kinds of cultures. Where Lawrence of Arabia realized only one aspect of his intense personality, first in action and then in literature, van der Post has realized many. And the many roles he has played in active life are celebrated in the many incidents of his different books and are defined by the many names by which he has been called. The real objection to the nickname "Laurens of Abyssinia" is that he has lived in many countries of the world, and that even his name has changed a little in each. Where Lawrence of Arabia sought to return to the anonymity of "Aircraftsman Shaw" after the war, and failing that, died, "Laurens of Abyssinia" has continued to act in many new roles. The variety of the many names by which he has been known suggests the variety and richness of his personality. When Frank Debenham introduced him to the readers of his book, *Kalahari Sand,* he called him "Van," but added that "you will soon find other names for him, as I did." Although no others have used the name, "Van," it may serve as a compromise between the informal first name and the formal last name, and also emphasize his distinctive Dutch and Afrikaner ancestry.

In South Africa the last name, van der Post, was wholly native, and fitted both his ancestral role of farmer, and his early professional role of journalist. But later in England, when he volunteered for training as commando at the beginning of the war, his old friend Desmond Young called "van der Post" an "exotic name." As he gradually rose in rank, "Colonel van der Post" became his official title, and the picture on the dust jacket of his first novel after the war showed him in army uniform capped with a commando's beret. Colonel van der Post he has remained for formal purposes, although typically in *Venture to the Interior* he emphasized that he was really only "a half-colonel." But his first name has always been more common, and when Desmond Young told of meeting him in Abyssinia, he spoke of his old friend, "Laurie." Meanwhile the Afrikaner pronunciation of "Laurens" had been anglicized by his English friends, such as William Plomer and Roy Campbell, so that the phonetic "Lawrence" naturally became associated with "Abyssinia." And in England he had already been naturalized for social and informal purposes as "Lawrence," although he remained "Laurens van der Post" by formal South African citizenship.

After the war his many journeys of exploration to the different countries of the interior of Africa brought him into close association with many native peoples, and perhaps it is the quality of his close relationship with these which most distinguishes his personality. More than any other white man he has been able to establish spontaneous friendship and rapport with natives, who in turn have called him by his first name. But because they could seldom pronounce it properly, "Laurens" has become many different things on different tongues.

Among the Bushmen of the Kalahari "Laurens" became "Moren." Without formal warning of this, he has described his close friendship with the "tame Bushman," Dabé in *The Heart of the Hunter*. This "detribalized" Bushman, who lived uneasily on the physical border between the white man's civilization and the native desert, felt an instinctive attraction to this Afrikaner, who had also become "detribalized" both nationally and culturally. And perhaps the most eloquent chapter of this moving book is entitled "Go in Peace, Moren." The intense inner feeling between the white man and the Bushman is perfectly conveyed by the latter's final exclamation: "Auck, Moren! You are really a great skelm!" The archaic word "skelm," or "rascal," suggests the trans-cultural understanding between the two. For only in South Africa has the word "skelm" remained colloquial, where it is often used to address animals. And to the Bushman the animal has often been the most intimate of friends. When Dabé called the white man "a great skelm," he welcomed him into the primeval brotherhood of all living things.

Laurens Jan van der Post, Colonel van der Post, Van, Laurens, Lawrence, Laurie, and Moren—all these names have actually been used. They suggest the different relationships into which he has entered with different types of people in the different cultures of the world. There may be many more. He is also "John Lawrence," a real character in the actual drama of history, but created by the author's imagination for a specific practical purpose.

Beyond history, however, his different "personae," or the different dramatic characters created by his fictional imagination, also share some of these actual names. The actual "John Lawrence" becomes the fictional officer who finally succeeds in understanding and communicating with his Japanese captors. And Jacques Celliers, the fictional South African officer who symbolically succeeds in this by means of action, complements him. Johann van Bredepoel embodies fictionally the earlier irresolution of the author during the Great Depression. David Michaeljohn embodies his earlier homesickness while in English "exile," while Pierre de Beauvilliers incarnates his active ideal of explorer and soldier, combined with sensitive anthropologist. Meanwhile the passive narrator of *The Face Beside the Fire* and the nameless narrator of *The Seed and the Sower* complete the list. But the most memorable of these fictional names is perhaps that applied to the fictional John Lawrence by one of his fictional Japanese captors: in order to symbolize the triumph of human understanding over wartime hatred, the Japanese addresses Lawrence as "Rorensu-San."

All these names, actual and fictional, suggest the different aspects of the personality of the author. This personality, both in its historic actuality and its fictional imagination, dominates his writing. It has been realized by a long life of action, but it has also been projected and unified by a lifelong work of the creative imagination. It is, in the deepest sense, a work of art, as truly as was Whitman's more artificially imagined "Myself." From his own "many avatars ascending," van der Post's unified self gives meaning to his many and different books.

The unity of this multifaceted personality, both actual and ideal, is seldom stated explicitly. But it is suggested by the author's Introduction to *The Heart of the Hunter*: "I had a feeling that I was possibly the only person who could start this kind of interpretation; who could be this kind of improvised rope-bridge over the deep abyss between modern man and the first person of Africa, until the real engineers with proper suspension bridges should come along." A kind of rope bridge over the abyss between modern civilization and primitive culture—between Europe and Africa—he has served as mediator and interpreter between the two.

### III   *The African Myth*

The autobiographical personality of the author which dominates both his life and his books, has taken its form from "the master pattern at work within me"—the pattern of African life. In earlier parts of this book we have observed the historical patterns of this life and analyzed the individual elements of the personality. But beyond history and individual personality, every country or continent imagines for itself some national myth to explain its originality and to define its identity. Van der Post has collected the aboriginal myths of the African Bushmen and has described the opposing myth-images of the white queen and the black titan. But what, exactly, is "the master pattern" behind these myths? What is the unity behind African diversity?

No single African myth exists, of course, in the usual sense of the word. Yet many African writers and thinkers in recent years have attempted to imagine some ideal identity to give pattern to their African life and history. Ezekiel Mphahlele has written a book on *The African Image*, although, as he cheerfully admits, this "can remain but a glorious myth."[3] He has also summarized the various attempts by politicians to celebrate "The African Personality," as a step toward realizing some ideal pan-Africanism. And Leopold Senghor, perhaps the most articulate spokesman of Black Africa, has defined *"négritude"* as "emotion." But *"négritude,"* "The African Image," and "The African Personality," have all been imagined to define the identity of Black Africa, only. Their exclusive pattern seems to reject "the master pattern at work within me," which van der Post has both experienced and described. His "African Myth" is both multiracial and inclusive.

Black Africans have often rejected the myth of the white queen described by Rider Haggard, because it seems to symbolize an exclusive, white imperialism. The imperious queen, who dominates her black subjects by the force of her superior will, does sometimes smack of white supremacy. Like the white god of the Aztecs, whom their ancient prophets worshiped before history brought the white conquistadors, this mythical white queen has appeared to incarnate the white man's superiority complex. As if to apologize for this mythical superiority, van der Post exclaims: "We white men started with a very unfair psychological advantage, when we went to Africa, going there in the image of Whiteness."

But whiteness of skin, both in fact and in the imagination of Black Africans, is superficial. Accepting the universal symbolism of Black and White, Africans have applied it only inwardly, saying of their Zulu tyrant, Chaka, that "he had a black heart." To tyrannical white rulers, they have also imputed black hearts. The white queen, painted by aboriginal black artists on the rock walls of the Kalahari, did not prophesy the future rule of the white race, but the rule of an inward goodness or beauty.

This mythical white queen of Africa comes closer to universal acceptance when she symbolizes the principle of civilization, as opposed to savagery. Rider Haggard imagined her as descended from an ancient Egyptian queen, and the legend of an unknown African civilization, mothered by some queen of Egypt or by the Ethiopian Queen of Sheba, and surviving timelessly in the savage interior, has been widespread. This imagined civilization would bridge the abyss between ancient Egyptian civilization and modern colonial civilization and would create for African history an ideal continuity. To support this, modern anthropologists have hypothesized the migrations of half-civilized races from upper Egypt into the basins of the Niger and the Congo. More recently Black Africans have turned again to Egypt, both for political support and for ideal unity. Leopold Senghor has even advocated the teaching of ancient Egyptian to modern African students, rather than of ancient European languages like Greek and Latin. The white queen also symbolizes the continuity of the principle of civilization in Africa.

Yet this ideal of continuous civilization in Africa remains unreal. Senghor's suggestion that ancient Egyptian should be taught to modern Africans seems almost as fantastic as Rider Haggard's genealogy of Ayesha's ancestry, and her timeless vitality. For history has never been continuous in Africa because writing has not survived the migrations. Whatever peoples wandered from Egypt into the Niger and the Congo basins did not bring Egyptian hieroglyphics with them. The principle of civilization remained buried, symbolically, under the Egyptian pyramids.

Whether the white queen symbolizes imperial rule, or the principle of civilization, or the feminine quality of kindness, she constitutes only one half of the African myth. Opposing her in whatever role she assumes is the mythical black titan, Adamastor. When the white queen appears as the imperial Ayesha, the black titan assumes "a most fiendish and terrifying expression." When she appears as the sea nymph rising from foam and spray, the black titan becomes a tormented Prometheus, unjustly denied her love by the arbitrary gods. When she appears as the lady of the lotus flower, the titan becomes the ideal of *négritude*, or the universal principle of emotion which her beauty calls forth. But each of these opposing images presupposes the other. Each can be terrifying, or tormented, or beautiful by turns, depending on the character assumed by the other.

The "master pattern" of African life and myth, as van der Post has described it, is that in which each character presupposes its opposite. Although white queen and black titan oppose each other, they have need of each other: they coexist in a kind of symbiotic relationship. When Egyptian civilization first built its geometrical pyramids, it needed its multitude of black slaves. And in recent times the black rulers of the newly independent nations of Africa have needed their white engineers. As with nations, so with individuals: in all his life and writings van der Post has most valued and best realized that very quality of deep feeling which "is" *négritude*. Similarly Mphahlele has analyzed "The African Image" and has criticized the "mysticism" of van der Post's writing, by means of the very civilized tools of logical analysis which he first learned from his South African professors.

The inner meaning of the myth of the white queen and black titan is not that of white supremacy, or the triumph of civilization, or even the power of beauty, but rather the recurrent opposition and interrelation of black and white, actual and ideal. This African myth does not prophesy the coming of a white god incarnated in white conquerors, nor the return of the principle of civilization from its historic Egyptian sources. It "prophesies," rather, a truth beyond time and history—or, at least, beyond the recorded time of history. The mythical white queen and black titan act out the timeless drama of rule and revolt, civilization and savagery, gods and titans. And they project this drama of eternal recurrence upon the "lost world" which existed before history—and, indeed, before humanity—began. In this sense the white queen Ayesha is truly deathless, and her story timeless.

But if the African myth does not "prophesy" historic events, it does project a pattern which history has often seemed to follow. And perhaps the most spectacular realization of this pattern has occurred recently, not in fact, but in scientific hypothesis. Since *The Dark Eye* was written, archaeologists have discovered many hominid remains in Africa which seem to verify the hypothesis that *homo sapiens* first developed his most distinctively human characteristics in ancient Africa, and moreover that the modern Bushman represents the partial survival of a very old prehistoric race and culture. If the Afrikaners believed that they would discover the Garden of Eden in the Interior, modern archaeologists now believe that evolution actually produced *homo sapiens* in this African interior. An American author, Robert Ardrey, has recently summarized the archaeological evidence supporting this hypothesis under the title of *African Genesis*. Thus "the African Myth" has projected the pattern, not only of modern historic events, but also of modern scientific hypotheses concerning prehistoric events.

The master pattern of African life, embodied first in the fantasies of myth and fiction, and then in the patterns of history and the hypotheses of science, explains much of the fascination of Africa for the modern mind. Van der Post's most imaginative books often seem to prophesy the actual problems of today as well as the ideal speculations of modern scientists and scholars. His lifelong concern with the aboriginal Bushman, in particular, prefigures the interest of modern scientists in this unique people. For the Bushman's prehistoric ancestors seem to have evolved a

human intelligence and culture which predate anything known
in Europe or Asia: many millenniums before the earliest Egyptians, these ancestors flourished.

The significance of "The Lost World of the Kalahari" is twofold. The survival of the Bushman emphasizes the multiracial
nature of African life. "Though gone from the land," writes van
der Post, "he still stalked life in the mixed blood of the coloured
peoples as subtly as he ever stalked the multitudinous game of
Africa. . . . Here a strain of Bushman blood would give an otherwise good Bantu face an odd Mongolian slant, there turn a good
central African black into an apricot yellow." And the modern
American anthropologist, Loren Eiseley, also emphasizes that
"Africa is not a black man's continent in the way we are inclined
to think . . . it has its genetically strange variants, its racial deviants whose blood stream is no longer traceable."[4] To identify
Africa with "*négritude*," therefore, is as false as to identify civilization with white supremacy.

Most important, "The Lost World of the Kalahari" was the
site, both actual and symbolic, of the genesis of *homo sapiens*.
Well-preserved skulls recently discovered in widely separated
caves in South Africa indicate the existence of a race even
greater in brain capacity and more refined in "dentition" than
the modern white race. As Eiseley reconstructs them, "they are
related in some dim manner to the Kalahari Bushman. . . .The
Bushman's forerunners might have stepped with Weena [H. G.
Wells's fictional man of the future] out of the future eras of the
Time Machine."[5] That is to say, the first scientifically identifiable
members of *homo sapiens* lived untold millenniums ago in Southern Africa, but their prehistoric culture was overwhelmed by
forces we can only conjecture. From the very beginning of time,
the symbolic white queen (of human intelligence, civilization,
or the feminine principle of gentleness) has confronted the symbolic black titan (of anthropoid strength, savagery, or the masculine principle of aggression) in South Africa.

"The African Myth" does not imagine any single story of white
queen and black titan, nor does it imagine any continuous history of African civilization. It suggests, rather, the recurrent
confrontation of white queen and black titan, of civilization and
savagery, and their eternal interrelation. The myth is not timely,
but timeless—it imagines eternal recurrence. It all happened be-

fore history began; it happened again in the rise and fall of
Egyptian civilization; it is happening today in new patterns.

"Africa is old in the longest measure of time on earth," writes
van der Post. "Indeed, those of us who are born in Africa are
born with a sense of this old oldness deep within us." If the
African myth is that of eternal recurrence, its historic symbol
is the ancient Egyptian serpent with its tail in its mouth—the
universal symbol of eternity. This hieroglyphic symbol implies
both destruction and creation, its head eternally swallowing its
tail, digesting the future out of its own dissolution. In mythology,
it appears as the dread serpent Ouroboros, which eternally en-
circles the earth. But in whatever form or fiction, it always includes its opposite.

An even better symbol of this African myth might, perhaps,
be the Bushman god, Kwammanga, as van der Post describes
him in *The Heart of the Hunter*. He is born of the rainbow, son
of black cloud and white sun shining through rain. And he is
married to the daughter of another Bushman god, the All-
Devourer. After black storm, white light, but dispersed (like
the Bushman's blood) through all the colors of the rainbow and
all the races of man.

## IV  *Africa Within*

An "African Myth" (as has been said) does not exist: there
is no unified mythology common to all African peoples. Black
Africans often reject the white man's myths, and they fail to
agree among their own. Although van der Post has described
many individual myths and has suggested fresh interpretations
of them, he has never attempted to define a single "African
Myth." In collecting his descriptions and interpretations, this
book has attempted to define "the master pattern" whose unity
he has only suggested. But even if no single myth exists, a coherent system of philosophy and psychology lies behind his
interpretations. His *Dark Eye* suggests this, developing many
new ideas, and his uncollected essays and lectures develop
original interpretations of great value.

*The Dark Eye* pays homage to Jean Jacques Rousseau, whose
"concept of 'the noble savage' has haunted the imagination of
artists, poets and social reformers ever since." And it is possible
to read *The Lost World of the Kalahari* as a celebration of

Rousseau's noble savage. But throughout his life and writing, van der Post has treated "the savage" realistically. He has met the classical criticism of the armchair romanticist by exposing himself repeatedly to hardship and danger in order to live closely with "savages," and he has reported their more ignoble as well as their admirable characteristics. Even more important, he has entered into the minds and hearts of the Bushmen in order to describe the inner "nobility" of many of those customs which might seem ignoble to unsympathetic observers. Not only has he observed "the savage" with the accuracy of the scientist, but he has described him with the intuitive sympathy of the artist.

He has proved himself an active explorer and an artistic writer. But giving motive to his exploration and giving urgency to his writing is a deeply felt moral conviction. His Introduction to *The Dark Eye* addresses "my black and coloured countrymen who may read this book," in order to "explain my use of the words 'primitive' and 'civilized'." The words describe a "general difference which undeniably exists between indigenous and European man in Africa," but they do not imply the superiority of one to the other. Rather the opposite: "We need the good that is in the values of 'primitive' man in Africa." His books attempt to describe these primitive values, and to argue their continued relevance to the world of today. Of course Rousseau was motivated by much the same moral purpose, but writing from an armchair about imaginary savages, he often confused the issues.

Between the romantic speculations of Rousseau and the realistic explorations of van der Post lie the psychological theories of Carl Jung (to whom *The Dark Eye* was first addressed). Jung has supplied a theoretical framework which gives pattern to Rousseau's imaginings and gives purpose to van der Post's explorations. For the fact remains: although the "savage" (whether noble or ignoble) still exists in Africa, his old way of life has been doomed by modern civilization (whether progress or imperialism). The best that van der Post could hope to accomplish, practically, for the Bushmen was to persuade his government to protect them on some "park" or "reservation," much as it has protected its wild animals. But the "primitive" or "savage" values of the Bushmen may still be recognized in the human psyche, and their continued relevance to civilized man accepted. Jung's concepts of "the collective unconscious" and "the shadow" emphasize their psychological universality, even though recognizing their practical danger. Supposing that actual savagery should cease to exist, its values would remain.

All van der Post's books about Africa describe two separate Africas—the external continent which he has so repeatedly explored, and the African heart of darkness which lies within the soul of man. It is his emphasis on the Africa within which raises his books of physical exploration to universal significance.

The psychological theories of Jung have lent themselves well to the literary purposes of van der Post, and to his interpretation of the African scene. Where Freud had described men's complex delusions as individual and abnormal, caused by personal fixations and confusions, Jung described them as normal in origin, caused by the unconscious suppression of instincts which had once been normal in earlier cultures. Moreover, Jung used the literary techniques of personification and dramatization to express his psychological ideas. Where Freud had described the instinctual self as an abstract "Id," Jung personified it (or part of it) as "the shadow," and dramatized its origin in "the collective unconscious." Sometimes Jung functioned more as a literary critic than a scientist, showing how literary myths described psychological experiences, and how even realistic literature might be interpreted in psychological terms.

Jung's concept of "the shadow" thus proved particularly relevant to the interpretation of Africa, but it was also ambiguous. Defining this "shadow" as the embodiment of all those "dark" impulses which civilized man has rejected in his own life and consciousness, Jung suggested how "the shadow" has reappeared in many different guises. In public literature he has often taken the form of the dark villain performing acts of violence, and in private dreams he has performed acts of immorality. Usually he has seemed wholly evil and immoral, although sometimes merely primitive. But always—both in conscious literature and in the dream symbolism of all people—he has been a mysterious figure of darkness.

In *The Dark Eye* van der Post described the universal nature of those repressions which in modern times have resulted in the "darkening of the eye" of subjected peoples everywhere, but particularly in Africa, where the white man's repression of the native has often been extreme. But his phrase, "the dark eye," suggested only the outward manifestation of an inward "darkness." It had nothing to do with the outer darkness of a man's skin. These two darknesses, however, had become confused. In a 1957 lecture (and pamphlet) entitled "Race Prejudice as Self-Rejection," he made clear this confusion, and the reasons for it. Then he went on to develop original ideas of his own.[6]

Although the phenomenon of inward darkness described in *The Dark Eye* is world-wide, having been fostered by the politics of colonialism, it has been intensified in Africa, compounded by a psychological confusion. The symbolic "heart of darkness" has been projected upon Africa, partly because black Africans have seemed to incarnate all the dark impulses of man: their *"négritude"* has seemed symbolic as well as physical. Irrationally, the white man has attributed to the Negro "the black heart" and "the dark eye" because of his black skin. The black man has become the projection, not of the actual Negro, but of the white man's fear of blackness. In rejecting this black man, whom he has unconsciously identified with his own psychological "shadow," the white man has rejected part of his own self. Racial prejudice has therefore become confused and intensified by the white man's fear of his own shadow self.

This idea—and the clear recognition and practical application of it—underlies all van der Post's life and writing. It underlies his interpretation of *apartheid* in South Africa: "In my own country, it is not the black man as such that we are legislating against. It is the projection of the rejection inside ourselves of the natural man." And it explains his own repeated explorations of physical Africa: "I discovered that I traveled in Africa because it brought me to unknown places in my own uncomprehended spirit which I could not have reached in any other manner." The conscious recognition of this idea and the acceptance of all its implications seems to him all-important: "The problem was and today is the acceptance of the image of the dark, of the darkness in ourselves." Therefore his exploration of "the heart of darkness"—both physical and psychological, and his emphasis on the image of darkness—both in Africa and in the heart of man. But how are we to recognize and accept this darkness, which white civilization has repressed from its consciousness and rejected?

In answer van der Post offers an original symbolic interpretation of "the Christian myth." The Bible (he says) narrates two great "journeys": that of the Old Testament, and that of the New. The first tells how primitive man was expelled from "the Garden" of innocence, and fell into the bondage of Egypt and established civilization. But he escaped from Egypt into the desert, where the basis of a new civilization was revealed to him (the tablets of the Law). His descendants used this Law to establish a new civilization in the Promised Land. But after a time the Law became legalistic, and the new civilization corrupt. Prophets foretold the coming of a new Messiah who would lead beyond the limits of the old Law.

The second Biblical myth begins with the coming of God to earth as man. But He is not recognized, and the new Messiah is born outside the Law. He, too, is forced to flee from his native land, and is taken into Egypt. He too returns, and after a sojourn in the wilderness, reveals the basis of a new civilization—the law of Love, which is beyond the old Law. But this new law is rejected by the guardians of the old, and eventually His disciples are forced to flee to alien lands. There the New Testament of Love becomes accepted. But this gospel, in its turn, has become institutionalized and corrupted, like the old Law. It is time for a third "journey."

Both the Old Testament of Law and the New Testament of Love involved the fact of rejection. The old Law rejected the criminal, while the gospel of Love—although forgiving the criminal—rejected his all-too-human impulses as sinful. By rejecting man's dark nature, and repressing his dark impulses to the subconscious, Christianity fostered civilization, but denied half of man's nature. It alienated him from his "shadow" self. At this point, van der Post makes an extraordinary statement of faith:

I feel there has also been a third great discovery in the mechanism of man. It links up closely with what is implied in the process of man becoming God. This discovery owes an enormous amount to Carl Gustav Jung. He has found that by delving into dreams and into the rejected aspects of the psyche, there is found the godlike mythological activity in the human being, a sort of master image which, if you can get hold of it, can deal with the mechanism of rejection.

In each of us there is a transcendent image that can reconcile these opposites, bring them together and make it possible for us to move on again. This is the phase at which we stand today.

This statement of faith—made informally in a lecture many years ago, awkwardly phrased, and not repeated or reprinted since—does not, perhaps, belong to literature. But it is important for many other reasons. It affirms a belief in the perfectibility of man which relates van der Post to other writers of other countries and other times. It defines the personal faith which has given motive and direction both to his life and to his writing. And finally, it projects the outlines of a major idea toward which other contemporary writers have been moving.

"The process of man becoming God" is, of course, an original teaching of Christianity: "Be ye therefore perfect, even as your Father which is in heaven is perfect." But it is a teaching which sophisticated modern man has often rejected. Only occasionally, in times of sudden growth and impending change, men have sometimes believed that "all things are possible." So the American Transcendentalists in 1840 affirmed their "several adherence to a new hope, . . . a greater trust in the nature and resources of man, than the laws or the popular opinions will well allow."[7] Linking the idealism of van der Post to the earlier idealism of Emerson and Whitman, his phrase also links religious faith to the recurrent experiences of modern history.

On the level of individual experience, also, van der Post is here affirming the faith which has guided his own actual life. This idealism has never seemed to him merely philosophical, but rather practical. In his own experience "the mechanism of rejection" came first, and he spent the first half of his life learning to deal with the "dark" experiences of exile and alienation. Only gradually did he grope toward the "third great discovery in the mechanism of man"—which he credits here to Carl Gustav Jung. If his emphasis on this "third discovery" seems extreme, it is because his own experience has convinced him of its magnitude; and if he attributes too much credit to Jung, it is because he found in this philosophy a pattern which gave meaning to his own earlier random experiences.

Moreover, his own biography, and his literary description of it in successive books, has been much more active and less abstract than that of Jung—or of the earlier American Transcendentalists. Where Jung's autobiography could only describe his inward experiences, and where Emerson's Transcendentalism seemed a product of "Solitude" more than "Society," van der Post has both experienced and celebrated the life of action. Since a "God-like perfection" has always been easier to imagine in the inner world than in the outer, and since it has been easier to realize on paper than in practice, van der Post's affirmation of the possibility of "man becoming God," and his extreme praise of the inward-living Jung seem all the more remarkable.

Finally, his broad interpretation of the Christian "myth," with its two "Testaments" of "Law" and "Love," has proved prophetic. A Freudian psychiatrist, Bruno Bettelheim, has recently described his own experiences in treating emotionally disturbed children in a book entitled *Love Is Not Enough*. No amount of love could effect the cure of the rejected and disturbed children under his care—only the gradual discovery of the origins of their rejection in actual experience, and the bringing of this to consciousness. Christian Love was not enough to deal with the "mechanism of rejection"—only a "delving into dreams and into the rejected aspects of the psyche" could sometimes produce wholeness.

The clinical exploration of the mechanism of rejection by modern psychiatry is paralleled by the philosophical exploration of the meanings of myth by Jung and his followers. Erich Neumann, a disciple of Jung and a friend of van der Post, has interpreted the earliest mythology of Egypt as a symbolic description of "The Origins of Consciousness." Ouroboros, the circular serpent of Egypt eternally holding his tail in his mouth, symbolizes the primitive unity of human consciousness before conscious knowledge had been separated from unconscious dream—objective fact from subjective fantasy. For the primitive has always been characterized by the fusion (and confusion) of fact and fantasy. Civilization began in Egypt and the Near East when this symbolic serpent unwound itself and entered into nature, tempting primitive man with the gift of conscious knowledge. This origin of consciousness, however, which made civilization possible, also exiled primitive man from the Garden of innocence and destroyed his unity with the nature of things.

As the growth of consciousness made possible the intellectual accumulation of science and the political organization of civilization—first under the Old Testament of Law, and later under the New Testament of Love—man's power over nature increased, while his unity with nature decreased. The conscious rejection of his natural self caused increasing conflict—both politically within civilized societies, and psychologically within man's self. Man's feeling of exile increased, and with it the mental illness which seems the hallmark of civilization.

But, as Erich Neumann has also suggested, the primordial Egyptian serpent Ouroboros not only symbolizes a "non-differentiated state of union" in the beginning of things. Ouroboros also symbolizes "the creative impulse of the new beginning; it is the 'wheel that rolls of itself,' the initial rotatory movement in the upward spiral of evolution."[8] In the modern world, and particularly in Africa, it symbolizes a return to the primitive origins of civilization, and to the dark unconscious. It explains van der Post's own physical explorations of "the lost world" of primitive Africa and his ideal explorations of primitive myth. Ouroboros, the Egyptian symbol of eternal recurrence, may also provide the "sort of master image which, if we can get hold of it, can deal with the mechanism of rejection." By exploring the primitive country of Africa, and the psychological country of the heart of darkness, van der Post has realized much of the meaning of African myth in modern literature, with its "creative impulse of the new beginning."

## V  *Conclusion*

Autobiography and myth—the physical adventures of the author and the symbolic descriptions of the heart of darkness—these two extremes of literary form best characterize van der Post's achievement. On the one hand, his books have appealed to a host of readers interested simply in geographical exploration and adventure. On the other hand, they have aroused the intense enthusiasm of groups interested in psychological insight and intercultural understanding. Any final estimate must include both extremes.

In a recent conversation the name of van der Post was mentioned to a British teacher and editor, who expressed immediate enthusiasm. He was preparing an anthology of the literature of travel and exploration, and had included passages from *Venture to the Interior* and *The Lost World of the Kalahari.* "The best descriptions of the wild country of Africa that I know," he said. But he was totally unaware of other books by the author, and—more surprising—was unaware of any psychological insights or anthropological ideas in these. For their vivid descriptions of physical explorations, the excellence of these books has been widely recognized.

Meanwhile, other readers of opposite tastes have found in the same books a different fascination. Depth psychologists, both professional and amateur, have praised them. They have appealed not only to the followers of Carl Jung but to a host of readers concerned with the psychological and anthropological understanding of racial and cultural problems. The American professor visiting Tokyo, who chanced to pick up a German translation of *A Bar of Shadow* and found in it the best explanation of Japanese psychology that he knew, is typical. Van der Post's books have been welcomed by men of different professions and interests in different countries of the world, both for their unique insights into the problems of race and culture, and for their autobiographical explorations of more personal problems.

Although his books have appealed separately to readers interested only in physical exploration, and to those interested only in psychological exploration, their unique success lies in their fusion of these two genres or types of writing. *Venture* has become a classic in the literature of exploration, because of this double purpose and double vision. Exploring both the physical and the psychological worlds, these books achieve a unique excellence.

But of course there have been criticisms. Most obviously, the author began as a reporter and has returned frequently to the profession of journalism. Not only has he worked on different newspapers, but many of his articles (including one whole book) have been written for magazines: although *A View of All the Russias* is journalism at its best, it is still journalism. And more important, the easy colloquial style of the journalist has entered into the writing of his other books. At best, this style brings the author to life as a speaking presence on the printed page; at worst, it expresses vague ideas in careless language. But, of course, the same criticism applies equally to Mark Twain.

Another criticism emphasizes an opposite element of style. His attempt to intensify the literary effect of narratives and descriptions has sometimes resulted in overwriting. Although his fictional storms often achieve genuine grandeur, they sometimes become too literary—"the cavalry of the great army of cloud" rides too hard and too often. The resulting hint of artifice becomes more insistent when the storms sweep down at the end of each chapter, as if to underline the stormy emotions of the characters.

These faults of style may be considered occasional, resulting from a too-enthusiastic overwriting, or a too-careless under-editing. But they also point to a more fundamental criticism, which has often been directed at his work as a whole—that of "mysticism." For it is in the very nature of mysticism to teach the "one-ness" of things, and to describe by means of metaphor and symbol the unity of apparent opposites—of man and nature, storms of anger and storms of electricity, the dark heart of man and the heart of darkness in Africa. In this sense, of course, all symbolic writing is mystical, and all poetic metaphor implicitly preaches the philosophy of unity.

The particular interest and the particular excellence of van der Post's writing is that, at its best, his mysticism is wholly functional and intrinsic. His early novel, *In A Province,* was purely realistic. And when he first read Carl Jung before the war, he found Jung "too mystical for my taste." Subsequently, in the tragic years of the world war, and particularly in the dark years of his own torture and imprisonment by the Japanese, he suffered a kind of conversion or change of heart, motivated in part by the very realistic need to understand the enemy if he (and his fellow prisoners) were to survive at all. Since the war, all his books have expressed different degrees of this mysticism, both in their literary style and in their explicit philosophy. It is perhaps significant that the most mystical of these books, and the one most guilty of overwriting is *The Seed and the Sower,* which focuses most sharply upon these experiences as prisoner-of-war.

This mysticism has also contributed to the problem of form. In his attempt to describe new experiences and to express new meanings, he has often abandoned the traditional forms of literature. After a first book which followed the pattern of the well-made novel, he sought new patterns to interpret new ideas. This resulted in the radically new form of *Venture to the Interior,* in the fragmentations of form in *The Dark Eye* and *The Seed and the Sower*, and in the frank abandonment of traditional form in *The Heart of the Hunter*. In earlier chapters we have examined the different degrees of success achieved by the different books in their struggle with this problem. Certainly some of them have achieved imperfect success because of their imperfections of form.

Such criticism seems more important to the traditional literary critic than to the general reader. Many other literary explorers have achieved their most telling effects by rejecting traditional forms. In these books, the extremes of autobiography and myth—of experienced fact and imagined symbol—often seem to project their union beyond the limits of the individual volumes. Each describes fragments of autobiography and suggests outlines of myth which eventually join to create a larger autobiographical legend. And this autobiographical myth (as suggested in the Preface) may well be the greatest creation of the author.

To the literary critic, the skill with which this autobiographical myth has been communicated in the books seems most important: readers have often experienced as complete an imaginative realization of the personality of the author as did earlier readers of Whitman's "Song of Myself." But where Whitman's autobiographical "self" had been more than half fiction, van der Post's has been essentially fact: his autobiography is of a piece with his biography. To the general reader this historical reality may seem even more significant than the degree of literary skill with which it has been communicated.

But beyond literary—and even beyond historical—criticism, the final fascination of these books may well lie in their projection of a new philosophy of life embodied in a new type of autobiographical personality. This philosophy is not abstract, but emphasizes action; it is not exclusive, but emphasizes total participation. The autobiography narrates the experience of all kinds of life, in association with all types of people, in all the different countries of the earth. It is the story of the man whose actual experience and ideal imagination have combined to make him an international citizen, at home in all the world.

# Notes and References

## Chapter One

1. William Plomer, *Turbott Wolfe* (London, 1965), Introduction by L. van der Post, p. 51.
2. Letter dated Feb. 4, 1965.
3. See William Plomer, *Cecil Rhodes* (New York, 1933).
4. "Profile" published in the *Cape Times* c.1960. Quoted from a copy supplied by Mr. van der Post, exact date not determined.
5. From Introduction to *Turbott Wolfe* (see note 1), p. 29.
6. Van der Post in Introduction (see above), and Plomer in *Double Lives* (New York, 1956).
7. Plomer, *Double Lives*, p. 193.
8. Few copies of *Voorslag* have survived. One is available in the University of Texas library. Complete files of all eleven issues are preserved in the public libraries of Johannesburg and Durban.
9. Desmond Young, *Try Anything Twice* (London, 1963), p. 222.
10. *Ibid.*, pp. 225-27.
11. Letter dated Feb. 4, 1965.
12. Letter dated May 11, 1964.

## Chapter Two

1. Plomer, *Double Lives*, p. 201.
2. *Ibid.*, p. 208.
3. Stephen Spender, *The Destructive Element* (London, 1935), pp. 236-51.
4. Letter dated May 11, 1964.
5. L. van der Post, *The Face Beside the Fire* (New York, 1953), p. 123.
6. Desmond Young, *Try Anything Twice* (London, 1963), pp. 275-76.
7. Article by L. van der Post, *Holiday* (Oct., 1961), p. 54.
8. Quoted in I. L. Baker, *Laurens van der Post: Venture to the Interior* (Bath, England, 1963), p. 9.
9. Quoted in Young, *Try Anything Twice*, p. 276, from Frank Foster, *Comrades In Bondage*.

## Chapter Three

1. Letter dated May 11, 1964.

2. Carl Gustav Jung, *Memories, Dreams, Reflections* (New York, 1962).

3. Frank Debenham, *Kalahari Sand* (London, 1953), p. 42.

4. *Ibid.*, pp. 41-42.

5. *Ibid.*, p. 71.

6. "Profile" published in the *Cape Times* 1960.

7. Pamphlet by L. van der Post, *Race Prejudice as Self-Rejection*, published by Workshop for Cultural Democracy (New York, 1957). Out of print.

8. Pamphlet by L. van der Post, "Intuition, Intellect and the Racial Question," published by The Myrin Institute, Adelphi University (New York, 1964), p. 5.

9. *Ibid.*, p. 24.

## Chapter Four

1. Loren Eiseley, *The Immense Journey* (New York, 1957).

## Chapter Five

1. Ezekiel Mphahlele, *The African Image* (New York, 1962), p. 128.

## Chapter Six

1. T. E. Lawrence, *Seven Pillars of Wisdom*, reprinted in *The Essential T. E. Lawrence*, ed. David Garnett (New York, 1963), pp. 208-9.

2. Letter dated May 11, 1964.

3. Mphahlele, *The African Image*, p. 19.

4. Eiseley, *The Immense Journey*, p. 133.

5. *Ibid.*, p. 134.

6. Most of the following quotations are from the pamphlet, *Race Prejudice as Self-Rejection*.

7. Emerson's Introduction to *The Dial*, July, 1840.

8. Erich Neumann, *The Origins of Consciousness* (New York, 1962), vol. I, p. 18.

# Selected Bibliography

## PRIMARY SOURCES
### A. Books

*In A Province*. New York: William Morrow & Co., 1934. London: The Hogarth Press, 1934.

*Venture to the Interior*. New York: William Morrow & Company, 1951. London: The Hogarth Press, 1952. New York: Compass Books, 1961 (paperback).

*The Face Beside the Fire*. New York: William Morrow & Co., 1953. London: The Hogarth Press, 1953.

*A Bar of Shadow*. London: The Hogarth Press, 1954. New York: William Morrow & Co., 1956.

*Flamingo Feather*. New York: William Morrow & Co., 1955. London: The Hogarth Press, 1955.

*The Dark Eye in Africa*. New York: William Morrow & Co., 1955. London: The Hogarth Press, 1955. Reissued with new author's "Introduction, 1960." New York: Apollo Editions, 1960 (paperback).

*The Lost World of the Kalahari*. New York: William Morrow & Co., 1958. London: The Hogarth Press, 1958. New York: Apollo Editions, 1963 (paperback).

*The Heart of the Hunter*. New York: William Morrow & Co., 1961. London: The Hogarth Press, 1961. New York: Apollo Editions, 1966 (paperback).

*The Seed and the Sower*. New York: William Morrow & Co., 1963. London: The Hogarth Press, 1963.

*A View of All the Russias*. New York: William Morrow & Co., 1964. English title: *Journey Into Russia*. London: The Hogarth Press, 1964.

*The Hunter and the Whale*. New York: William Morrow & Co., 1967. London: The Hogarth Press, 1967.

### B. Articles, Pamphlets, Introductions

This list is highly selective. Articles, reviews, and poems published in South African newspapers are not included. Pamphlets and recordings limited to private circulation are not included.

"*Kuns Ontwikkeling in Afrikaans*," *Voorslag*, Durban (July, 1926), 39-43.

"*Nimrods van die See*," *Voorslag*, Durban (August, 1926), 40-45.

"South Africa in the Melting Pot," *The Realist*, London, II (Nov., 1929), 254-64.

"Personal Experiences Of Primitive Africa," *Aus dem Jahresbericht, Psychologischer Club,* Zurich (Nov., 1951).

"A Bar of Shadow: A Story," *The Cornhill,* London, vol. 166, pp. 42-67 (Spring, 1952). (Later published as book, 1954).

"Africa," *Holiday,* New York, XV (March, 1954), 34-50 and 134-42.

"About the Bushmen in Africa," *Psychologischer Club,* Zurich (March, 1955).

"The Primitive Pattern in South Africa," *Eranos Jahrbuch,* Zurich, 1957, pp. 417-54.

*Race Prejudice as Self-Rejection,* Workshop for Cultural Democracy, New York, 1957. Original pamphlet, out of print.

"Journey Through a Floating World" [Japan], *Holiday,* New York (October, 1961), pp. 54-74 and 121-33.

*Patterns of Renewal.* Pendle Hill, Wallingford, Penna., 1962. Original pamphlet.

*Intuition, Intellect and the Racial Question.* Myrin Institute, Garden City, L. I., New York, 1964. Original pamphlet.

"Introduction," *The Nile,* by Eliot Elisofon. New York: The Viking Press, 1964.

"Introduction," *Turbott Wolfe,* by William Plomer. London: The Hogarth Press, 1965. A 46-page reminiscence of South African life, combining autobiography with literary criticism.

SECONDARY SOURCES

Baker, I. L. *Laurens van der Post: Venture to the Interior.* Bath, England: James Brodie Ltd., no date (1963). "Notes on Chosen English Texts."

Debenham, Frank. *Kalahari Sand.* London: Bell, 1953. Detailed account of expedition with van der Post in 1950.

Mphahlele, Ezekiel. *The African Image.* New York: Frederick A. Praeger, 1962. "Chapter 7: The White Man's Literary Image of the Non-White in Fiction" includes discussion of van der Post.

Plomer, William. *Double Lives.* New York: The Noonday Press, 1956. (New edition. First published in England, 1943.) Autobiography, including detailed accounts of *Voorslag,* and of voyage to Japan.

Spender, Stephen. *The Destructive Element.* London: J. Cape, 1935. "Chapter XIV: Upward, Kafka and van der Post."

*Times Literary Supplement,* London, March 15, 1963. "Nation to Nation." An essay-review discussing all van der Post's books to date, describing him as a writer of international literature.

Young, Desmond. *All the Best Years.* New York: Harper and Row, 1961. English title: *Try Anything Twice.* London: Hamish Hamilton, 1963. Autobiography, including accounts of editing the *Cape Times* with van der Post in 1930, and of meeting in Abyssinia in 1941.

# Index

Abyssinia, 18, 37, 45, 46, 48, 87, 90, 132, 133, 134, 135, 136, 137, 138, 139.
Adamastor, 17
*African Genesis,* 144
*African Image, The,* 106, 141
Anderson, Hans C., 125
Ardrey, Robert, 144
Ascona, 61
Atkinson, Brooks, 77
*Atlantic Monthly,* 63

Baker, I. L., 63
*Bar of Shadow,* 50, 53, 62, 66, 76, 120, 154
Batavia (see Djakarta)
Bettelheim, Bruno, 152
Boer War, 15, 19, 21, 22, 45
British Broadcasting Co., 71
Brook Farm, 42
Browne, Sir Thomas, 82, 87
Burton, Sir Richard, 134
Byron, Lord, 30

California, University of, 7, 71
Calvinism, 19, 20, 108, 113
Camoens, Luis, 16, 18
Campbell, Roy, 29, 30, 32, 139
*Cape Times, The,* 23, 33, 34, 40, 47, 68
Capricorn, Society of, 36, 57, 67
Chaka, 142
China, 51, 77, 78, 104
Churchill, W., 56
Clemens, S. (Mark Twain), 21, 154
Conrad, Joseph, 40, 62, 105
*Cornhill, The,* 66
*Cry, The Beloved Country,* 106

Dante, 71
*Dark Eye in Africa, The,* 15, 18, 22, 24, 35, 47, 54, 57, 61, 62, 67-70, 74, 79, 82, *86-91,* 97, 105, 106, 131, 133, 144, 146, 147, 148, 149, 156
Debenham, Frank, 64, 65, 93, 94, 138

*Dial, The,* 29
Dinesen, Isak, 84
Djakarta, 53
Donne, John, 137
*Double Lives,* 30
Doughty, Charles, 134

Egypt, 17, 62, 142, 143, 150, 152, 153
Eisley, Loren, 80, 145
Eliot, T. S., 30, 43
Elisofon, Eliot, 70
Emerson, R. W., 29, 130, 151
*Eranos Jahrbuch,* 72
Ethiopia (see Abyssinia)

*Face Beside the Fire, The,* 22, 24, 35, 40, 44, 66, 105, 107, *111-115,* 124, 140
*Flamingo Feather,* 43, 69-70, 105, 107, *115-119,* 124
Forster, E. M., 40
*Following the Equator,* 21
Foster, Frank, 53
Freud, Sigmund, 40, 148

Gama, Vasco da, 16, 17
Gandhi, Mohandas, 56
Giffard (see van der Post)
Grey College School, 24, 28, 32
Grieg, Edvard, 126

Haggard, H. Rider, 17, 69, 85, 115, 116, 136, 142
Hague, The, 53, 54
Hardy, Thomas, 63
*Harmless People, The,* 93
*Heart of the Hunter, The,* 27, 62, 74, *96-101,* 139, 141, 146, 156
Hertzog, J. B. M., 33
Hopkins, G. M., 59, 83
*Holiday,* 70, 72, 74, 76, 102
*Hunter and the Whale, The,* 31, 106, *124-130*

Ibsen, H., 125
*In A Province,* 34, 40, 41, 42, 43, 79,

161